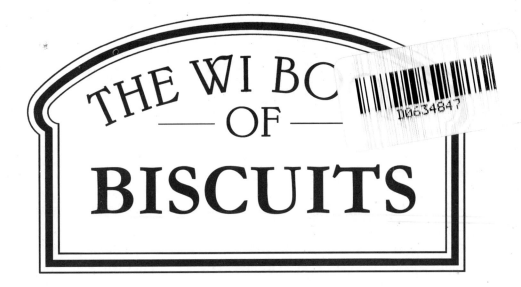

THE WI BOOK
OF
BISCUITS

Jill Brand

WI BOOKS

Copyright © National Federation of Women's Institutes
This edition 2000 published by WI Books

in association with Stable Ltd
Glebe House, Church Street,
Crediton, Devon EX17 2AF

Illustrated by Michael Lye

British Library Cataloguing in Publication Data.
A CIP catalogue record for this book is available from the British Library.

ISBN 0 947990 08 9

Printed and bound in Great Britain by Short Run Press Ltd, Exeter, Devon

Note for Showing

If you are intending to use any of the recipes in this book for Schedules for Shows, remember to consult an up-to-date copy of *On With the Show*.

CONTENTS

CONTENTS

CONTENTS

INTRODUCTION

Biscuits are a great temptation all through the day. The mouth-watering tastes in this very special collection will more than match the tantalising aroma wafting from your oven. Even better, these are all quick and easy to make.

The previous edition of the *WI Book of Biscuits* has been a best-seller for 10 years. Many new recipes have now been added but we have kept the favourites from the original book. We believe temptation should be encouraged!

TYPES OF BISCUIT

The recipes have been divided into simple sections according to the general type of biscuit as follows. There is also a section on **Savoury Biscuits**.

1. **Cookies**
   These are usually made from softer doughs shaped using spoons, the palm of the hand, sliced from a roll or piped. The texture can be soft and cake-like or crisp. Part of the charm of home-made cookies is their often irregular shape.

2. **Flapjacks and Traybakes**
   These are cooked in tins which are usually base-lined to make turning out easier. At the end of baking mark out the shape required and then cut when completely cool.

3. **Sweet Biscuits**

These are usually rolled and cut. If you find the dough difficult to handle try chilling it slightly before rolling out. Try to use the minimum amount of flour on the surface when rolling out the dough and try to keep an even pressure on the rolling pin to ensure even thin biscuits. Remember to dust off the excess flour before baking.

4. **Microwave only**

A few recipes have been added for microwave cookery. These should only be cooked with the microwave. Don't try to adapt these to an ordinary oven.

GENERAL GUIDANCE

1. If the recipe requires melting ingredients together use a gentle heat so that the mixture is not overheated.

2. For best results when baking use a flat baking tray without high sides as these prevent proper browning. Always space the oven shelves evenly so the air can circulate properly and if cooking on more than one shelf in electric or gas ovens (not fan ovens) the lower tray may need moving to the higher position to complete the cooking.

3. Always leave space on the trays between the biscuits and cookies to enable them to keep their shape. Do not join them together.

4. When baked the biscuits and cookies should be left to cool on the baking tray before removing with a flat wide spatula to cooling racks to cool completely. Do not overlap when cooling.

5. To store your biscuits line an airtight container with non-stick paper and place a sheet of paper between each layer. If space allows store different types of biscuits and cookies separately.

6. If the biscuits have a filling sandwich them together just before serving to avoid loss of crispness.

Enjoy the product of your own baking!

COOKIES

ALMOND WAFERS

150 g (5 oz) butter
150 g (5 oz) caster sugar
80 g (3 oz) plain flour

80 g (3 oz) chopped flaked almonds
extra caster sugar for sprinkling

1. Cream butter and sugar together until light and fluffy.
2. Stir in the flour and almonds. Mix well to form a soft dough.
3. Place spoonfuls of the dough onto greased baking trays.
4. Bake 200°C, 400°F, Gas 6, fan oven 180°C, for 8–12 mins until golden and crisp.
5. Allow to cool. Sprinkle with caster sugar.

ALMOND COCOROONS

2 medium egg whites
80 g (3 oz) desiccated coconut
40 g (1¹/₂ oz) ground almonds

115 g (4 oz) caster sugar
rice paper

1. Whisk the egg whites until stiff.
2. Mix the coconut, ground almonds and sugar together and fold them lightly into the whisked egg.
3. Place the mixture in small rounds about 10 ml (2 tsp) each on rice paper on baking trays.
4. Bake 160°C, 325°F, Gas 3, fan oven 140°C, for 20–25 mins.

ANZAC COOKIES

Traditional Australian cookies.

100 g (3¹/₂ oz) rolled oats
150 g (5 oz) plain wholemeal flour
115 g (4 oz) light brown sugar
115 g (4 oz) dark brown sugar
50 g (2 oz) desiccated coconut

25 g (1 oz) glacé cherries, chopped
115 g (4 oz) margarine
30 ml (2 tbsp) clear honey
2.5 ml (¹/₂ tsp) bicarbonate of soda *and*
15 ml (1 tbsp) water – mixed together

1. In a large bowl place the oats, flour, sugars, coconut and cherries. Blend together.
2. Melt the margarine and honey gently together. Stir into oat mixture. Add bicarbonate liquid and mix together ensuring even coating.
3. Place teaspoons of the mixture onto greased baking trays leaving space between each.
4. Bake 180°C, 355°F, Gas 4, fan oven 160°C, for 15–25 mins until set and golden.
5. Allow to cool on wire rack.

BRANDY SNAPS

A crisp biscuit which can also be served with ice cream.

50 g (2 oz) butter
50 g (2 oz) caster sugar
30 ml (2 tbsp) golden syrup
50 g (2 oz) plain flour, sifted

2.5 ml (¹/₂ tsp) ground ginger
5 ml (1 tsp) brandy
grated zest of ¹/₂ lemon
150 ml (5 fl oz) whipped cream

1. Melt the butter, sugar and syrup in a small saucepan over a gentle heat.
2. Remove from the heat, stir in the remaining ingredients and mix well.
3. Place small spoonfuls of mixture on greased and lined baking trays allowing space for spreading.
4. Bake 180°C, 355°F, Gas 4, fan oven 160°C, for 8–12 mins.
5. Remove from oven, allow to cool for one minute then loosen with palette knife and roll round greased handles of wooden spoons.
6. Leave to set then gently twist to remove. Fill with whipped double cream to serve.

Note: To make baskets mould around base of greased teacups.

BASIC DROP COOKIES

80 g (3 oz) margarine
80 g (3 oz) caster sugar
1 medium egg
225 g (8 oz) plain flour

2.5 ml (¹/2 tsp) baking powder
45 ml (3 tbsp) milk
2.5 ml (¹/2 tsp) vanilla essence

1. Cream the fat and sugar together then add the beaten egg.
2. Sieve the flour and baking powder together. Add to the creamed mixture alternately with the milk and vanilla essence. (Not all the milk may be needed as the mixture must not be too soft.)
3. Drop teaspoonfuls of the mixture onto greased trays leaving room for the biscuits to spread.
4. Bake 180°C, 355°F, Gas 4, fan oven 160°C, for 10–20 mins.

VARIATIONS:
i. Substitute soft brown sugar to make a light brown cookie.
ii. Add 80 g (3 oz) dried fruit and 25 g (1 oz) chopped nuts.
iii. Add 5 ml (1 tsp) powdered cinnamon to the dry mixture.
iv. Substitute 15 ml (1 tbsp) cocoa for 25 g (1 oz) flour.

Note:
All the cookies may be iced and decorated in many ways.

CINNAMON COOKIES

Lovely with a cup of coffee.

115 g (4 oz) butter
200 g (7 oz) soft brown sugar
2 medium eggs
45 ml (3 tbsp) milk
275 g (10 oz) plain flour

2.5 ml (¹/2 tsp) bicarbonate of soda
10 ml (2 tsp) cinnamon
115 g (4 oz) sultanas
50 g (2 oz) pecan nuts, chopped

1. In a bowl beat together the butter and sugar until creamy. Add the eggs and beat well.
2. Mix in the remaining ingredients stirring to a soft dough.
3. Place spoonfuls of the mixture onto greased baking trays. Flatten slightly.
4. Bake 190°C, 375°F, Gas 5, fan oven 170°C, for 15–20 mins until lightly golden in colour.

DOUBLE CHOCOLATE CHIP COOKIES

A real must for the true chocoholic – white and milk chocolate together. Makes 20.

115 g (4 oz) butter, softened
50 g (2 oz) caster sugar
115 g (4 oz) soft brown sugar
1 medium egg, beaten
2.5 ml (^{1}/2 tsp) vanilla essence

175 g (6 oz) plain flour
5 ml (1 tsp) baking powder
115 g (4 oz) plain chocolate drops
115 g (4 oz) white chocolate drops

1. In a large mixing bowl cream together the butter and sugars until light and fluffy.
2. Gradually add the beaten egg, mixing after each addition, then beat in the vanilla essence.
3. Sift the flour and baking powder into the bowl and fold in thoroughly.
4. Fold in the chocolate drops then place heaped teaspoonfuls of the dough 5 cm (2 ins) apart on the greased baking trays.
5. Bake 180°C, 355°F, Gas 4, fan oven 160°C, for 15–20 mins until golden.
6. Allow to cool on the baking sheet for 5 mins then transfer to a cooling rack to cool completely.

VARIATION:
Leave out half the chocolate and use chopped nuts to make up same weight.

DATE AND WALNUT COOKIES

225 g (8 oz) margarine
175 g (6 oz) caster sugar
2 medium eggs, beaten
275 g (10 oz) self-raising flour, sieved
15 ml (1 tbsp) cinnamon

150 g (5 oz) walnuts, roughly chopped
150 g (5 oz) stoned dates, roughly chopped
75 ml (5 tbsp) milk

1. In a bowl cream the margarine and sugar together until light and fluffy.
2. Beat in the eggs, stir in flour, cinnamon, walnuts and dates mixing well. Gradually add the milk to form a dropping consistency.
3. Place heaped spoonfuls of the mixture onto greased baking trays and slightly flatten.
4. Bake 190°C, 375°F, Gas 5, fan oven 170°C, for 15–25 mins until lightly golden.
5. Cool on baking trays for 5 mins before placing on rack to cool completely.

AUNTIE DOT'S COOKIES

80 g (3 oz) butter or margarine
80 g (3 oz) caster sugar
80 g (3 oz) self-raising flour

half a medium egg
80 g (3 oz) raisins
cornflakes

1. Cream the fat and sugar together until creamy.
2. Stir in the flour and about half a beaten egg to make a very stiff dough.
3. Add the raisins.
4. Roll teaspoonfuls of the mixture into balls then roll them in cornflakes.
5. Place them on greased baking trays leaving plenty of room for them to spread.
6. Bake 180°C, 355°F, Gas 4, fan oven 160°C, for 12–15 mins.

CHOCOLATE CHERRY COOKIES

Makes 18–20.

115 g (4 oz) softened butter
50 g (2 oz) caster sugar
2.5 ml ($1/2$ tsp) vanilla essence

25 g (1 oz) glacé cherries
25 g (1 oz) plain chocolate
115 g (4 oz) plain flour

1. Cream the butter and sugar together and add the vanilla essence.
2. Chop the cherries and the chocolate finely and add to the mixture. Stir in the flour.
3. Place 18–20 teaspoonfuls of the mixture on well-greased baking trays leaving space for the biscuits to spread.
4. Bake 190°C, 375°F, Gas 5, fan oven 170°C, for 15–20 mins.

COFFEE WALNUT COOKIES

115 g (4 oz) butter
50 g (2 oz) caster sugar
115 g (4 oz) plain flour

50 g (2 oz) chopped walnuts
10 ml (2 tsp) instant coffee powder

1. Cream the butter and sugar together then add the rest of the ingredients.
2. Place small teaspoonfuls of the mixture on greased baking trays leaving plenty of room for the biscuits to spread.
3. Bake 190°C, 375°F, Gas 5, fan oven 170°C, for 15–20 mins.

COFFEE KISSES

175 g (6 oz) self-raising flour
80 g (3 oz) caster sugar
80 g (3 oz) margarine
1 medium egg, beaten

10 ml (2 tsp) instant coffee powder,
dissolved in 15 ml (1 tbsp)
boiling water

To finish:
butter icing (for ingredients and method see Lancashire Nuts p.14)

1. Sieve flour into a bowl. Add sugar and rub in the margarine until the mixture resembles breadcrumbs.
2. Stir in the egg and coffee mixture. Mix well.
3. Place balls the size of walnuts onto greased baking trays.
4. Bake 180°C, 355°F, Gas 4, fan oven 160°C, for 12–15 mins until puffy and set.
5. Allow to cool slightly before placing on cooling racks to cool completely.
6. To finish use butter icing to sandwich together.

VARIATION:
Flavour the butter icing with cocoa powder instead of vanilla essence to produce 'Mocha Kisses'.

CHOCOLATE DELIGHTS

A crunchy chocolate cookie ideal with coffee. My nieces thought these were delicious spread with melted chocolate. Makes 24.

175 g (6 oz) butter
50 g (2 oz) light brown sugar
115 g (4 oz) plain chocolate

175 g (6 oz) plain flour, sieved
80 g (3 oz) cornflakes, finely crushed
15 ml (1 tbsp) cocoa

1. Beat the butter and sugar together until well mixed.
2. Melt the chocolate in a bowl over hot water. Allow to cool then beat into butter and sugar.
3. Stir in the flour, cornflakes and cocoa.
4. Place teaspoonfuls of mixture onto greased baking trays allowing room for spreading.
5. Bake 180°C, 355°F, Gas 4, fan oven 160°C, for 15–20 mins. Allow the cookies to cool for 10 mins before removing to cooling rack.

GREEK COOKIES

These are usually served at Christmas. Makes approx. 40.

225 g (8 oz) butter
80 g (3 oz) caster sugar
30 ml (2 tbsp) ouzo
1 medium egg yolk
1.25 ml ($^{1}/_{4}$ tsp) vanilla essence

275 g (10 oz) plain flour
2.5 ml ($^{1}/_{2}$ tsp) baking powder
40 whole cloves
icing sugar
rosewater

1. Cream the butter and sugar. Beat in the ouzo, egg yolk and vanilla essence.
2. Sift the flour and baking powder and add to the mixture.
3. Mix well to make a firm dough.
4. Form rounded teaspoonfuls of the dough into balls and place on baking trays lined with baking parchment.
5. Flatten slightly and spike each cookie with a clove.
6. Bake 190°C, 375°F, Gas 5, fan oven 170°C, for 20 mins.
7. Transfer the biscuits immediately to a cooling rack. While still hot sprinkle with icing sugar and rosewater.

LANCASHIRE NUTS

115 g (4 oz) butter
115 g (4 oz) caster sugar
1 medium egg

115 g (4 oz) plain flour
115 g (4 oz) cornflour
15 ml (1 tbsp) baking powder

Filling:
50 g (2 oz) butter
115 g (4 oz) icing sugar

few drops vanilla essence

For the biscuits:
1. Cream the butter and sugar. Add the egg and beat them together.
2. Add all the dry ingredients. Mix to a paste.
3. Place teaspoonfuls of the dough on greased baking trays.
4. Bake 180°C, 355°F, Gas 4, fan oven 160°C, for 8–10 mins until golden.

For the filling:
5. Cream the butter until soft. Gradually add the sieved icing sugar and cream together. Add the vanilla essence and beat well.
6. When the biscuits are cold sandwich them together in pairs with the filling.

CRESTON DROPS

115 g (4 oz) butter
50 g (2 oz) caster sugar
2 medium eggs
3 squares chocolate, melted
115 g (4 oz) chopped walnuts

115 g (4 oz) raisins
225 g (8 oz) plain flour
5 ml (1 tsp) salt
2.5 ml ($\frac{1}{2}$ tsp) bicarbonate of soda
90 ml (6 tbsp) milk

1. Cream the butter and sugar together until creamy.
2. Add the eggs then the melted chocolate, nuts and raisins.
3. Sieve the flour with the salt and bicarbonate of soda and add them to the mixture alternately with the milk.
4. Drop spoonfuls onto greased baking trays and flatten with a spoon.
5. Bake 200°C, 400°F, Gas 6, fan oven 180°C, for 10–15 mins.

MACAROONS

2 medium egg whites
115 g (4 oz) ground almonds
25 g (1 oz) ground rice
225 g (8 oz) caster sugar

rice paper
a few split almonds
egg white for glazing

1. Whisk egg whites until stiff. Fold in ground almonds, ground rice and sugar.
2. Line baking trays with rice paper. Place small heaps of the mixture on the baking trays. Space out so there is room to spread.
3. Top each one with a split almond and glaze with egg white.
4. Bake 180°C, 355°F, Gas 4, fan oven 160°C, for 25–30 mins.

WALNUT CRISPS

80 g (3 oz) margarine
225 g (8 oz) self-raising flour
225 g (8 oz) brown sugar

115 g (4 oz) plain chocolate
115 g (4 oz) walnuts chopped
1 medium egg

1. Rub the margarine into the flour and sugar. Break the chocolate into pieces and add together with the walnuts.
2. Bind the mixture with the egg.
3. Place small heaps of dough on a greased baking tray and flatten with a fork.
4. Bake 180°C, 355°F, Gas 4, fan oven 160°C, for 15–20 mins.

CARROT AND CINNAMON COOKIES

Lightly spiced cookies that have already become a proven success as a family favourite. Makes 24

115 g (4 oz) softened butter
115 g (4 oz) soft brown sugar
1 medium egg
60 ml (4 tbsp) marmalade
225 g (8 oz) carrots, peeled
    and grated

200 g (7 oz) plain flour
2.5 ml ($^{1}/_{2}$ tsp) baking powder
5 ml (1 tsp) ground cinnamon
80 g (3 oz) glacé cherries,
    finely chopped

1. Place the butter and sugar in a bowl and beat until soft and light.
2. Beat in the egg and the marmalade. Stir in the carrots.
3. Sift together the flour, baking powder and cinnamon. Stir into the creamed mixture. Add the cherries and mix thoroughly.
4. Place spoonfuls of the mixture on greased baking trays making sure there is room for the cookies to spread.
5. Bake 180°C, 355°F, Gas 4, fan oven 160°C, for 15–20 mins until lightly golden.
6. Allow to cool on a wire rack.

BARNSTAPLE GINGERBREADS

Similar to brandy snaps but these gingerbreads are served flat. They are good with ice cream. Makes 18.

50 g (2 oz) butter
50 g (2 oz) caster sugar
80 g (3 oz) golden syrup

5 ml (1 tsp) lemon juice
50 g (2 oz) plain flour, sieved
5 ml (1 tsp) ground ginger

1. Place the butter, sugar and syrup in a saucepan. Gently heat until the butter is melted and the sugar dissolved. Remove from heat.
2. Stir in the lemon juice, flour and ginger mixing well. Allow to cool.
3. Place level teaspoonfuls of the mixture onto greased baking trays with plenty of space between each.
4. Bake 180°C, 355°F, Gas 4, fan oven 160°C, for 10–12 mins until flat and golden.
5. Remove and allow to cool for 1–2 mins before removing to wire racks to cool completely.

MELTING MOMENTS

80 g (3 oz) margarine
25 g (1 oz) lard
80 g (3 oz) caster sugar
$^1/_2$ medium egg

2.5 ml ($^1/_2$ tsp) vanilla essence
150 g (5 oz) self-raising flour
50 g (2 oz) rolled oats
chopped glacé cherries

1. Cream the margarine, lard and sugar together until fluffy.
2. Beat in the egg and vanilla essence.
3. Stir in the flour mixing together.
4. Shape mixture into walnut sized balls and roll in oats to coat.
5. Place on lightly greased baking trays. Flatten slightly and place a small piece of the chopped cherries on each biscuit.
6. Bake 180°C, 355°F, Gas 4, fan oven 160°C, for 10–15 mins. Leave to cool on baking trays for 5 mins before placing on cooling racks.

FRUITY SNAPS

50 g (2 oz) sultanas
25 g (1 oz) caster sugar
50 g (2 oz) margarine

60 ml (4 tbsp) golden syrup
150 g (5 oz) self-raising flour

1. Place the sultanas, sugar, margarine and syrup in a pan and warm them over a low heat. Take care that the mixture does not overheat.
2. Remove it from the heat. Add the flour and beat well.
3. Place small tablespoonfuls of the mixture well apart on greased baking trays.
4. Bake 180°C, 355°F, Gas 4, fan oven 160°C, for 12–15 mins until golden brown.
5. Allow to set before removing from the trays but do not leave for too long or they will stick.

AMARETTI COOKIES

A cross between a cookie and a macaroon, delicious with fruit salad. Makes 12.

3 medium egg whites	**225 g (8 oz) caster sugar**
225 g (8 oz) ground almonds	**30 ml (2 tbsp) flaked almonds**

1. In a large bowl whisk the egg whites until frothy.
2. Stir in the ground almonds and sugar and mix well.
3. Divide mixture into equal sized balls. Shape and place on greased baking trays then flatten slightly.
4. Sprinkle with flaked almonds.
5. Bake 180°C, 355°F, Gas 4, fan oven 160°C, for 10–15 mins until puffy and pale golden.
6. Cool on a wire rack.

BARBARA'S COOKIES

Favourite recipe of Barbara Gill, a member of the NFWI's Board of Trustees.

115 g (4 oz) butter	**25 g (1 oz) glacé cherries, chopped**
115 g (4 oz) soft brown sugar	**175 g (6 oz) self-raising flour**
50 g (2 oz) golden syrup	**50 g (2 oz) wholemeal self-raising flour**
80 g (3 oz) potato, peeled	**2.5 ml (1/2 tsp) ground nutmeg**
and finely grated	**2.5 ml (1/2 tsp) ground mixed spice**
25 g (1 oz) flaked almonds, chopped	**2.5 ml (1/2 tsp) ground cinnamon**

1. In a bowl cream together the butter and sugar until light and fluffy.
2. Stir in the syrup, potato, nuts and cherries mixing well.
3. Sift together flours and spices. Fold into mixture and mix well.
4. Place mixture into the refrigerator for at least one hour.
5. Remove from fridge and place mixture on a well-floured surface. Roll into a sausage shape approx. 4 cm (1 1/2 ins) in diameter.
6. Using a sharp knife cut the mixture into 15 mm (1/2 inch) slices.
7. Place cookies on greased baking trays.
8. Bake 200°C, 400°F, Gas 6, fan oven 180°C, for 15–20 mins.

CHERRY AND COCONUT COOKIES

These cookies are guaranteed to melt in the mouth. They are packed with cherries. Makes 24.

175 g (6 oz) butter, softened
175 g (6 oz) caster sugar
1 medium egg, beaten
150 g (5 oz) desiccated coconut

5 ml (1 tsp) baking powder
225 g (8 oz) plain flour
115 g (4 oz) glacé cherries

1. Beat together the butter and caster sugar until light and fluffy. Add the beaten egg and coconut. Mix well.
2. Sift in the baking powder and flour. Fold in using a metal spoon.
3. Roughly chop the cherries and work into the mixture.
4. Form the mixture into 24 balls and place well apart on the greased baking trays. Press down lightly with the back of a fork.
5. Bake 180°C, 355°F, Gas 4, fan oven 160°C, for 15–20 mins until pale golden.
6. Transfer to wire rack to cool completely. Store in airtight container for up to one week.

CHUNKY CHOCOLATE COOKIES

A lovely chocolate and nut cookie. For an authentic cookie chop the chocolate and nuts roughly. Makes 24.

250 g (9 oz) butter, softened
150 g (5 oz) light muscovado sugar
250 g (9 oz) self-raising flour *and*
25 g (1 oz) cocoa – sieved together

60 ml (4 tbsp) milk
175 g (6 oz) plain chocolate,
    roughly chopped
50 g (2 oz) Brazil nuts,
    roughly chopped

1. In a bowl cream the butter and sugar until creamy and fluffy.
2. Stir in flour, cocoa, milk, chocolate and Brazil nuts. Mix well to form a soft dough.
3. Divide mixture into 24 equal sized pieces. Roll each into a ball and place on greased baking trays with space for spreading then flatten slightly.
4. Bake 180°C, 355°F, Gas 4, fan oven 160°C, for 15–25 mins until soft, puffy and golden. Cool on trays for 5–10 mins before transferring to wire rack to cool.

CORNISH GINGER FAIRINGS

115 g (4 oz) butter
115 g (4 oz) caster sugar
15 ml (1 tbsp) golden syrup

175 g (6 oz) self-raising flour
5 ml (1 tsp) ground ginger
pinch of bicarbonate of soda

1. Gently melt the butter, sugar and syrup in a pan.
2. Mix in the dry ingredients.
3. Roll the dough into small balls and place on greased baking trays.
4. Bake 200°C, 400°F, Gas 6, fan oven 180°C, for 10–15 mins until golden brown.

CHERRY SNOWBALLS

225 g (8 oz) butter
50 g (2 oz) icing sugar
225 g (8 oz) plain flour
115 g (4 oz) chopped walnuts

5 ml (1 tsp) vanilla essence
pinch of salt
glacé cherries
fine caster sugar for rolling

1. Cream the butter with the icing sugar until fluffy.
2. Add the rest of the ingredients except for the cherries and mix well.
3. Flatten teaspoonfuls of the dough in the palms of your hands.
4. Place a cherry on each circle and cover by pinching the dough up round it.
5. Roll into balls and place on a greased baking sheet.
6. Bake 160°C, 325°F, Gas 3, fan oven 140°C, for 30–35 mins.
7. While still warm roll the biscuits in fine caster sugar.

CHOCOLATE ALMOND COOKIES

115 g (4 oz) butter
150 g (5 oz) caster sugar
1 medium egg *and*
30 ml (2 tbsp) milk, beaten together

175 g (6 oz) self-raising flour, sieved
80 g (3 oz) chocolate chips
80 g (3 oz) chopped blanched almonds

1. Cream the butter and sugar until light. Beat in egg and milk.
2. Stir in flour, chocolate chips and nuts mixing well.
3. Shape into balls using floured hands. Place on lightly greased baking trays ensuring space between each and press down.
4. Bake 180°C, 355°F, Gas 4, fan oven 160°C, for 12–15 mins until crisp and set.

CHERRY GINGER COOKIES

There is a subtle ginger flavour to these cookies. Makes 20.

250 g (9 oz) softened butter
150 g (5 oz) soft brown sugar
150 g (5 oz) wholemeal
   self-raising flour

225 g (8 oz) rolled oats
200 g (7 oz) glacé cherries,
   roughly chopped
50 g (2 oz) glacé ginger, finely chopped

1. Beat together the butter and sugar until creamy.
2. Stir in the flour, oats, cherries and ginger mixing well to form a soft dough.
3. Divide the dough into 20 equal sized pieces. Shape into balls and place on greased baking trays allowing space to spread. Flatten slightly.
4. Bake 180°C, 355°F, Gas 4, fan oven 160°C, for 15–25 mins until golden and soft. Cool on trays before placing on racks to cool completely.

CHOCOLATE MOMENTS

Makes 12.

115 g (4 oz) butter
50 g (2 oz) caster sugar
1.25 ml (1/4 tsp) orange essence
115 g (4 oz) plain flour *and*
25 g (1 oz) cocoa powder – sieved together

115 g (4 oz) plain chocolate chips
50 g (2 oz) cornflakes, crushed lightly
6 glacé cherries, halved

1. Cream the butter, sugar and essence together until soft and creamy.
2. Add the flour, cocoa and chocolate chips mixing together to form a soft dough.
3. Divide the mixture into 12 equal portions.
4. Roll into balls then roll in cornflakes to coat evenly.
5. Place on baking trays. Flatten slightly then place a half cherry on top.
6. Bake 190°C, 375°F, Gas 5, fan oven 170°C, for 10–15 mins until puffy and set. Leave to cool on trays before cooling completely on wire racks.

'SMARTIES' COOKIES

Wonderful treat!

115 g (4 oz) butter
115 g (4 oz) dark brown sugar
50 g (2 oz) light brown sugar
1 medium egg, beaten

115 g (4 oz) wholemeal self-raising
 flour, sieved
115 g (4 oz) plain flour, sieved
115 g (4 oz) 'Smarties'
 (3 tubes approx.)

1. Cream butter and sugars together until light and fluffy.
2. Beat in egg.
3. Stir in flours and 'Smarties'.
4. Divide the mixture into walnut sized pieces then place on greased baking trays.
5. Bake 180°C, 355°F, Gas 4, fan oven 160°C, for 8–12 mins.

   VARIATION:
   Replace 'Smarties' with 115 g (4 oz) chocolate chips.

FREEZER COOKIES

Ideal for making to cook at a later time. Makes 30.

115 g (4 oz) margarine
175 g (6 oz) caster sugar
1 medium egg
200 g (7 oz) self-raising flour *and*
25 g (1 oz) cocoa powder – sieved together

50 g (2 oz) Brazil nuts, chopped
50 g (2 oz) chocolate chips
50 g (2 oz) glacé cherries, quartered

1. Cream the margarine and the sugar together until light and fluffy then beat in the egg.
2. Stir in the remaining ingredients and mix all together to form a soft dough.
3. Form the dough into a roll approx. 4 cm (1½ ins) round then wrap in greaseproof paper. Wrap tightly in foil and freeze. Defrost in fridge for 6 hours when required.
4. Slice the dough into 30 slices and place on lightly greased baking trays leaving room for cookies to spread.
5. Bake 180°C, 355°F, Gas 4, fan oven 160°C, for 15–20 mins.

CARDAMOM COOKIES

80 g (3 oz) icing sugar
225 g (8 oz) softened butter
225 g (8 oz) plain flour
50 g (2 oz) chopped walnuts

5 ml (1 tsp) almond essence
2.5 ml (^{1}/2 tsp) ground cardamom
pinch of salt
icing sugar to dredge

1. Sift the icing sugar.
2. Add the rest of the ingredients and blend to a firm mixture.
3. Shape the dough into 2.5 cm (1 inch) balls and place them spaced 5 cm (2 ins) apart on greased baking trays.
4. Bake 180°C, 355°F, Gas 4, fan oven 160°C, for 20 mins or golden brown.
5. Dredge the cookies with icing sugar before serving.

COCONUT CRISPS

225 g (8 oz) soft margarine
80 g (3 oz) icing sugar
few drops of vanilla essence

225 g (8 oz) self-raising flour
25 g (1 oz) desiccated coconut

1. Cream all the ingredients except for the coconut.
2. Form the mixture into small balls and roll in the coconut.
3. Place on greased baking trays.
4. Bake 160°C, 325°F, Gas 3, fan oven 140°C, for 15–20 mins until golden brown.

BUTTER COOKIES

175 g (6 oz) butter
115 g (4 oz) soft brown sugar
225 g (8 oz) plain flour

To roll:
25 g (1 oz) demerara sugar

1. Cream the butter and sugar until light in colour.
2. Blend in the flour and work the mixture to a smooth dough.
3. Divide and shape into two sausages then roll in the demerara sugar. Wrap in greaseproof paper.
4. Leave in the fridge until they are stiff (about 30 mins).
5. Cut into slices and place on greased trays.
6. Bake 180°C, 355°F, Gas 4, fan oven 160°C, for 15–20 mins.

CHOCOLATE MELTS

The staff at NFWI unit at Denman College named these. Makes approx. 28.

115 g (4 oz) milk chocolate
225 g (8 oz) soft margarine
50 g (2 oz) icing sugar
5 ml (1 tsp) vanilla essence

30 ml (2 tbsp) milk
225 g (8 oz) plain flour *and*
115 g (4 oz) cornflour *and*
2.5 ml (^{1}/2 tsp) baking powder – sieved together

1. In a bowl over hot water melt the chocolate then allow to cool.
2. Beat together margarine, sugar, melted chocolate, essence and milk.
3. Stir in sieved ingredients and mix to a soft dough.
4. Divide into approx. 28 walnut sized balls and place on lightly greased baking trays then flatten slightly.
5. Bake 190ºC, 375ºF, Gas 5, fan oven 170ºC for 15–20 mins until puffy and set. Leave to cool for 5 mins before removing to cooling racks.

CUMBERLAND SNAPS

115 g (4 oz) caster sugar
225 g (8 oz) margarine
30 ml (2 tbsp) golden syrup
5 ml (1 tsp) bicarbonate of soda

15 ml (1 tbsp) hot water
225 g (8 oz) plain flour
50 g (2 oz) rolled oats
5 ml (1 tsp) ground ginger

1. Melt the sugar, margarine and syrup over a low heat.
2. Dissolve the bicarbonate of soda in the hot water then mix together with all the other ingredients.
3. Roll the dough into small balls about the size of a walnut. Place on a greased tin.
4. Bake 160ºC, 325ºF, Gas 3, fan oven 140ºC, for 20–25 mins until golden brown.

FRUITY BRITTLES

150 g (5 oz) butter or margarine
115 g (4 oz) self-raising flour
115 g (4 oz) caster sugar
pinch of salt

115 g (4 oz) chopped mixed fruit
50 g (2 oz) chopped walnuts
1 medium egg
115 g (4 oz) crushed cornflakes

1. Rub the butter into the flour then mix in the sugar, salt, mixed fruit and chopped nuts.
2. Beat the egg and stir the mixture to form a dough.
3. Roll small pieces of the mixture in the crushed cornflakes.
4. Place on greased baking trays leaving room for them to spread.
5. Bake 200°C, 400°F, Gas 6, fan oven 180°C, for 10–15 mins.
6. Leave to cool for 5 mins before removing to cooling rack.

GIPSY CREAMS

50 g (2 oz) lard
50 g (2 oz) margarine
50 g (2 oz) caster sugar
115 g (4 oz) self-raising flour

50 g (2 oz) rolled oats
15 ml (1 tbsp) cocoa powder
10 ml (2 tsp) golden syrup dissolved in ...
15 ml (1 tsp) hot water

Filling:
25 g (1 oz) butter
50 g (2 oz) icing sugar

15 ml (1 tbsp) chocolate powder
few drops of vanilla essence

For the biscuits:
1. Cream together the lard, margarine and sugar then mix in all the other ingredients.
2. Roll the dough into balls about the size of a large cherry.
3. Place on greased baking trays. Flatten with fork which has been dipped in water.
4. Bake 180°C, 355°F, Gas 4, fan oven 160°C, for 20–25 mins.
5. Leave on trays to cool.

To make the filling:
6. Cream the butter until soft. Gradually add the sieved icing sugar and cream to a smooth consistency. Add the chocolate powder and vanilla essence and beat well.
7. When the biscuits are cold sandwich together in pairs with the filling.

GIPSY CRISPS

80 g (3 oz) cornflakes
225 g (8 oz) self-raising flour
115 g (4 oz) sugar
150 g (5 oz) margarine

30 ml (2 tbsp) golden syrup
5 ml (1 tsp) bicarbonate of soda
10 ml (2 tsp) boiling water

1. Crush the cornflakes and mix with the dry ingredients.
2. Melt the margarine and syrup and add to the dry mixture.
3. Dissolve bicarbonate of soda in the boiling water and add to the mixture.
4. Roll the dough into small round balls and place on greased baking trays.
5. Bake 150°C, 300°F, Gas 2, fan oven 130°C, for 20–25 mins.

GROUND RICE COOKIES

115 g (4 oz) margarine
115 g (4 oz) self-raising flour
115 g (4 oz) ground rice

115 g (4 oz) caster sugar
1 medium egg
caster sugar for coating

1. Rub the margarine into the mixed dry ingredients and blend into a dough with the beaten egg.
2. Roll the dough into small balls and dip in sugar.
3. Place on greased baking trays and flatten slightly with a fork.
4. Bake 180°C, 355°F, Gas 4, fan oven 160°C, for 15–20 mins.

PEANUT BUTTER COOKIES

15 ml (1 tbsp) peanut butter
grated rind of $1/2$ orange
50 g (2 oz) butter
45 ml (3 tbsp) light brown sugar

50 g (2 oz) caster sugar
1 medium egg
115 g (4 oz) self-raising flour

1. Cream peanut butter, orange rind, butter and sugars until light and fluffy.
2. Work in the beaten egg and stir in the flour to make a firm mixture.
3. Roll the dough into walnut sized pieces.
4. Place well apart on a greased baking tray.
5. Dip a fork in a little flour and press criss-cross lines on top of each one.
6. Bake 180°C, 355°F, Gas 4, fan oven 160°C, for 25–30 mins until puffy and golden brown.

NUT CRISPIES

Makes approx. 9.

25 g (1 oz) fine oatmeal
25 g (1 oz) wholemeal flour
25 g (1 oz) walnuts, chopped

25 g (1 oz) butter or margarine,
   softened
14 g (¹/2 oz) soft brown sugar

1. Mix all the ingredients together to form a dough.
2. Form into small balls. Place on greased baking trays then flatten with palm of the hand.
3. Bake 180°C, 355°F, Gas 4, fan oven 160°C, for 8–10 mins until golden.

ORANGE COCONUT CRISPS

Makes 15.

80 g (3 oz) butter or margarine
50 g (2 oz) caster sugar
zest & juice of 1 orange
50 g (2 oz) plain flour

25 g (1 oz) cornflour
pinch of salt
desiccated coconut

1. Cream together the fat and sugar until light and fluffy. Beat in the grated orange zest.
2. Add the sifted flour, cornflour and salt and mix to form a dough.
3. Shape dough into 15 small balls.
4. Brush with orange juice and roll in the coconut.
5. Place on a greased baking tray and flatten slightly.
6. Bake 180°C, 355°F, Gas 4, fan oven 160°C, for 15–20 mins.

PEANUT COOKIES

115 g (4 oz) soft margarine
115 g (4 oz) caster sugar

50 g (2 oz) salted peanuts
150 g (5 oz) self-raising flour

1. Cream the margarine and sugar together thoroughly.
2. Chop the nuts and stir them into the mixture with the flour.
3. Place walnut sized balls of the dough on a greased baking tray.
4. Bake 180°C, 355°F, Gas 4, fan oven 160°C, for 20–25 mins.

YO-YOs

175 g (6 oz) margarine
50 g (2 oz) icing sugar
175 g (6 oz) self-raising flour
50 g (2 oz) custard powder
2.5 ml ($^1/_2$ tsp) vanilla essence

Filling:
50 g (2 oz) butter
115 g (4 oz) icing sugar
2–3 drops vanilla essence

For the biscuits:
1. Cream the margarine and sugar. Stir in the flour and custard powder. Add the vanilla. Form to a dough.
2. Roll the dough into balls and place on baking trays. Mark with the back of a fork.
3. Bake 180°C, 355°F, Gas 4, fan oven 160°C, for 10–15 mins.
4. Cool on a wire tray.

To make the filling:
5. Cream the butter until soft. Gradually add the sieved icing sugar and cream together. Add the vanilla essence and beat the mixture well.
6. Sandwich the biscuits together with the filling.

NUT AND CHERRY COOKIES

The nuts and cherries give these delicious soft cookies a wonderfully crunchy finish. Makes 24.

225 g (8 oz) plain flour, sifted
80 g (3 oz) butter
115 g (4 oz) soft brown sugar
finely grated rind of an orange
1 medium egg, separated

60 ml (4 tbsp) milk
115 g (4 oz) finely chopped
  mixed nuts
12 glacé cherries, halved

1. Place flour in a bowl then rub the butter in until it resembles fine bread-crumbs. Add the sugar and orange rind.
2. Stir in the egg yolk and enough milk to give a firm dough.
3. Form into balls and dip in egg white then roll in the chopped nuts.
4. Place on lightly greased baking trays then flatten and place a half of a cherry on each.
5. Bake 180°C, 355°F, Gas 4, fan oven 160°C, for 20–25 mins until lightly browned.

CHORNS

Makes about 24.

80 g (3 oz) plain flour
115 g (4 oz) caster sugar
50 g (2 oz) desiccated coconut
50 g (2 oz) oats
25 g (1 oz) chopped mixed nuts

5 ml (1 tsp) bicarbonate of soda
30 ml (2 tbsp) golden syrup
115 g (4 oz) butter
45 ml (3 tbsp) water

1. Place in a bowl the flour, sugar, coconut, oats, nuts and bicarbonate of soda.
2. Melt the syrup and butter gently in a saucepan. Stir into the dry ingredients with the water and mix well.
3. Shape into balls and place on greased baking trays leaving space for spreading.
4. Bake 180°C, 355°F, Gas 4, fan oven 160°C, for 10–15 mins until golden in colour.
5. Allow to cool slightly before placing on wire racks to cool fully.

ST CLEMENT'S MELTAWAYS

A blend of flavours makes these interesting cookies. Makes 24.

225 g (8 oz) butter, softened
50 g (2 oz) icing sugar, sieved
finely grated rind of lemon
15 ml (1 tbsp) orange juice
225 g (8 oz) plain flour

Topping:
45 ml (3 tbsp) sieved
   lemon marmalade
45 ml (3 tbsp) icing sugar,
   mixed together with …
30 ml (2 tbsp) orange juice

1. Cream the butter and sugar together until creamy. Add the lemon rind and orange juice.
2. Stir in the flour and form to a soft dough.
3. Shape the mixture into balls and place on lightly greased baking trays.
4. Chill for one hour.
5. Bake 170°C, 340°C, Gas 3, fan oven 150°C, for 15–20 mins until pale golden.
6. Remove from oven, brush with the sieved marmalade then brush with icing mixture.
7. Return trays to the oven for 5 mins to allow the sugar to crystallize.
8. Cool on a wire rack.

FLAPJACKS AND TRAYBAKES

PRUNE AND COCONUT SQUARES

A good lunch box treat. Makes 16 squares.

80 g (3 oz) ready-to-eat prunes,
   chopped
rind and juice of 2 oranges
80 g (3 oz) butter
115 g (4 oz) dark brown sugar

2 medium eggs, beaten
115 g (4 oz) self-raising
   wholemeal flour *and*
50 g (2 oz) plain flour – sifted together

Topping:
2 medium eggs
60 ml (4 tbsp) honey

150 g (5 oz) desiccated coconut

1. Place the prunes, rind and juice of oranges into a small saucepan. Cook on a gentle heat until thick and soft. Allow to cool.
2. Cream the butter and sugar together. Beat in the eggs and fold in the flours.
3. Spread mixture into the base of a greased and lined 20 cm (8 ins) square tin.
4. Spread the prune mixture over the base.
5. **Topping:** Beat eggs together, stir in honey, then gradually add the coconut. Spread over prune mixture evenly.
6. Bake 180°C, 355°F, Gas 4, fan oven 160°C, 35–45 mins until evenly golden.
7. Leave to cool and then cut into squares.

APRICOT AND NUT SQUARES

Makes one 20 cm (8 ins) square which you can cut up into 9 pieces.

100 g (3¹/2 oz) rolled oats
115 g (4 oz) ready-to-eat apricots,
   chopped
80 g (3 oz) self-raising flour
50 g (2 oz) chopped mixed nuts

50 g (2 oz) chocolate, roughly chopped
150 g (5 oz) margarine
75 ml (5 tbsp) honey
50 g (2 oz) dark brown sugar

1. In a bowl place oats, apricots, flour, mixed nuts and chocolate. Mix well.
2. In a small saucepan place margarine, honey and sugar. Gently melt together. Stir into bowl of dry ingredients mixing well.
3. Place mixture into a lined and greased 20 cm (8 ins) square tin. Press down.
4. Bake 190°C, 375°F, Gas 5, fan oven 170°C, for 35–45 mins until dark golden. Leave to cool then cut into squares.

CHOCOLATE GINGER SHORTBREAD

A wonderful mix of chocolate and ginger. Makes 8 wedges.

150 g (5 oz) bar plain chocolate
225 g (8 oz) plain flour
5 ml (1 tsp) baking powder
5 ml (1 tsp) ground ginger
115 g (4 oz) butter
50 g (2 oz) soft dark brown sugar

25 g (1 oz) ground almonds
45 ml (3 tbsp) apricot jam
25 g (1 oz) preserved stem ginger,
   drained and finely chopped
50 g (2 oz) grated milk chocolate

1. In a bowl over hot water melt the chocolate and allow to cool.
2. Sieve together flour, baking powder and ginger. Rub in the butter until mixture resembles fine breadcrumbs.
3. Stir in sugar, almonds and melted chocolate mixing well together.
4. Knead lightly and press half of the mixture into a lightly greased and base-lined 20 cm (8 ins) round sandwich tin.
5. Brush with the warmed apricot jam and sprinkle with the chopped ginger and half the grated chocolate.
6. Press the other half of the mixture on top. Brush with jam and sprinkle with the remaining grated chocolate.
7. Bake 150°C, 300°F, Gas 2, fan oven 130°C, for 35–45 mins until cooked through. Allow to cool then cut into 8 wedges to serve.

CHOCOLATE PEPPERMINTY

115 g (4 oz) butter
50 g (2 oz) caster sugar
2.5 ml (¹/2 tsp) baking powder

15 ml (1 tbsp) drinking chocolate
115 g (4 oz) plain flour
80 g (3 oz) desiccated coconut

Filling:
80 g (3 oz) butter
80 g (3 oz) icing sugar
1.25 ml (¹/4 tsp) peppermint essence

Topping:
115 g (4 oz) cooking chocolate, melted

For the biscuit:
1. Cream the butter and sugar together until creamy.
2. Add the baking powder, drinking chocolate, flour and coconut.
3. Press the mixture into a Swiss roll tin.
4. Bake 190°C, 375°F, Gas 5, fan oven 170°C, for 15–20 mins until it is an even colour all over.
5. Leave to cool.

For the filling:
6. Cream the butter and icing sugar. Add the essence. Spread over the base.
7. Cover the layer of filling with the melted cooking chocolate. When the chocolate has set cut the biscuit into pieces.

OAT AND RAISIN TRIANGLES

These are a cross between flapjack and brownies. Crispy on the outside, soft and chewy in the centre. Makes 8.

80 g (3 oz) butter
115 g (4 oz) demerara sugar
30 ml (2 tbsp) golden syrup
175 g (6 oz) plain flour, sieved

25 g (1 oz) drinking chocolate powder, sieved
50 g (2 oz) rolled oats
50 g (2 oz) raisins
1 medium egg, beaten

1. In a saucepan place the butter, sugar and syrup. Heat gently until melted.
2. Stir in flour, drinking chocolate powder, oats, raisins and egg mixing well.
3. Transfer mixture into a greased and base-lined 20 cm (8 ins) sandwich tin.
4. Bake 180°C, 355°F, Gas 4, fan oven 160°C, for 25–30 mins.
5. Cut into 8 triangles when cooled.

SUNFLOWER CHOCOLATE FLAPJACKS

The combination of ingredients make this an interesting flapjack. Makes 24.

200 g (7 oz) margarine
80 g (3 oz) demerara sugar
30 ml (2 tbsp) golden syrup

275 g (10 oz) rolled oats
25 g (1 oz) sunflower seeds
115 g (4 oz) chocolate chips

1. Melt the margarine, sugar and syrup in a saucepan over a gentle heat. Remove from heat.
2. Stir in oats and sunflower seeds. Leave to cool for 10–15 mins then stir in the chocolate chips.
3. Place in a 30 x 23 cm (12 x 9 ins) tin lightly greased and base-lined.
4. Bake 160°C, 325°F, Gas 3, fan oven 140°C, for 30–40 mins until light golden brown. When cooked mark into 24 squares. Leave to cool in the tin.

CARAMEL BISCUITS

115 g (4 oz) butter
50 g (2 oz) caster sugar
175 g (6 oz) self-raising flour

Topping:
200 g (7 oz) chocolate

Caramel:
200 g (7 oz) tin of condensed milk
115 g (4 oz) margarine
50 g (2 oz) caster sugar
30 ml (2 tbsp) golden syrup
few drops of vanilla essence

For the biscuits:
1. Cream the butter and sugar together then mix in the flour.
2. Press the dough into a 30 x 20 cm (12 x 8 ins) baking tin.
3. Bake 180°C, 355°F, Gas 4, fan oven 160°C, for 15 mins until golden brown.
4. Leave to cool in the tin.

For the caramel:
5. Put all the ingredients in a pan and melt them over a gentle heat. Bring to the boil. Boil the mixture for 5 mins stirring all the time.
6. When cool pour over the base and leave to set.

For the topping:
7. Melt the chocolate in a bowl over a pan of simmering water and pour over the caramel.
8. When set cut into fingers.

COCONUT AND CHERRY SLICES

150 g (5 oz) cooking chocolate
50 g (2 oz) margarine
115 g (4 oz) caster sugar

1 medium egg
50 g (2 oz) glacé cherries
115 g (4 oz) desiccated coconut

1. Line a Swiss roll tin with foil. Melt the chocolate in a bowl over simmering water. Spread over the foil and leave to cool.
2. Cream the margarine and sugar. Beat in with the egg.
3. Chop the cherries and mix in with the coconut.
4. Spread this mixture over the cooled chocolate.
5. Bake 170°C, 340°F, Gas 3, fan oven 150°C, for 15–20 mins.
6. When cool cut into slices. Store in an airtight tin.

FIRELIGHTER BISCUITS

115 g (4 oz) margarine
15 ml (1 tbsp) golden syrup
225 g (8 oz) rolled oats

25 g (1 oz) desiccated coconut
115 g (4 oz) brown sugar
pinch of baking powder

1. Gently melt the margarine and syrup together. Add the dry ingredients and mix together thoroughly.
2. Press the dough into a Swiss roll tin to 1 cm (1/2 inch) thick.
3. Bake 180°C, 355°F, Gas 4, fan oven 160°C, for 20–30 mins.
4. Cut into fingers when it is cold.

COFFEE SHORTBREAD

A traditional recipe with a tang of coffee. Makes one 20 cm (8 ins) round.

80 g (3 oz) ground almonds
175 g (6 oz) plain flour
175 g (6 oz) softened butter

80 g (3 oz) soft brown sugar
30 ml (2 tbsp) coffee powder

1. Place all the ingredients in a bowl mixing together until a smooth dough is formed.
2. Evenly spread mixture into a base-lined 20 cm (8 ins) round sandwich tin.
3. Chill for one hour.
4. Bake 140°C, 285°F, Gas 1, fan oven 120°C, for 50–60 mins.

NUT AND FRUIT SHORTBREAD

175 g (6 oz) butter
80 g (3 oz) caster sugar
25 g (1 oz) ground rice
225 g (8 oz) plain flour

25 g (1 oz) glacé cherries, chopped
25 g (1 oz) angelica, chopped
50 g (2 oz) blanched almonds

1. Cream the butter and sugar. Add the ground rice and sieved flour.
2. Stir in the chopped cherries, angelica and half of the almonds.
3. Place the dough in a square-shaped tin and press the remainder of the almonds on the top.
4. Bake 180°C, 355°F, Gas 4, fan oven 160°C, for 30–40 mins.

RAISIN SHORTCAKE

Makes 8 wedges.

60 ml (4 tbsp) orange juice
115 g (4 oz) seedless raisins
115 g (4 oz) butter

175 g (5 oz) plain flour
50 g (2 oz) caster sugar

1. Put the orange juice and raisins into a pan and bring slowly to the boil. Leave to cool.
2. Rub the butter into the flour and sugar until the mixture resembles fine breadcrumbs.
3. Knead the dough well then divide into two equal rounds.
4. Put one on a greased baking tray and spread with the raisin mixture. Top with the second round and press firmly together.
5. Prick it well and mark into wedges.
6. Bake 180°C, 355°F, Gas 4, fan oven 160°C, for 40–50 mins.
7. Remove from the baking tray when cold and cut into wedges.

FRUIT OATIES

Makes 12 fingers.

175 g (6 oz) stoned prunes
115 g (4 oz) sultanas
finely grated zest and juice of 1 orange
90 ml (6 tbsp) water

225 g (8 oz) margarine
225 g (8 oz) plain wholemeal flour
225 g (8 oz) rolled oats
115 g (4 oz) soft dark brown sugar

1. Chop the prunes and place into a saucepan with the sultanas, orange zest and juice and water. Bring to the boil then gently simmer for 5–10 mins until the fruit is soft and the liquid is absorbed. Allow to cool.
2. Rub the margarine into the flour until the mixture resembles breadcrumbs then mix in the oats and sugar thoroughly.
3. Press half the mixture into an 18 x 28 cm (7 x 11 ins) greased and base-lined tin. Spread the fruit mixture evenly over the base mixture and cover with the remaining mixture. Press lightly down.
4. Bake 180°C, 355°F, Gas 4, fan oven 160°C, for 35–45 mins until lightly browned and set. When cooked allow to cool in tin then cut into fingers.

GERMAN ALMOND BISCUITS

225 g (8 oz) butter
175 g (6 oz) caster sugar
1 medium egg, beaten
115 g (4 oz) plain flour

115 g (4 oz) self-raising flour
raspberry jam
5 ml (1 tsp) sugar for glazing
flaked almonds

1. Cream the butter and sugar and add the beaten egg (keeping back a small quantity for glazing).
2. Stir in the flour and mix well.
3. Divide the mixture into two and cover the bottom of a well-greased round 18 cm (7 ins) tin with one half.
4. Spread with raspberry jam. Cover with the remaining mixture.
5. Add a teaspoonful of sugar to the remainder of the egg. Brush over the top and sprinkle with flaked almonds.
6. Bake 150°C, 300°F, Gas 2, fan oven 130°C, for 45 mins.
7. Cut into slices when almost cold.

Note:
Equally good without jam but mixture should then be spread over a larger tin.

TEBAY CRUNCH

225 g (8 oz) butter   350 g (12 oz) rolled oats
115 g (4 oz) caster sugar

1. Melt the butter and sugar in a pan. Add the oats gradually then mix them well together.
2. Turn the mixture into a greased dish.
3. Bake 180°C, 355°F, Gas 4, fan oven 160°C, for 15–20 mins until golden.
4. Cut into pieces when cold.

GRASMERE GINGERBREAD

450 g (1 lb) plain flour   10 ml (2 tsp) ground ginger
5 ml (1 tsp) bicarbonate of soda   225 g (8 oz) soft brown sugar
5 ml (1 tsp) cream of tartar   225 g (8 oz) butter or margarine

1. Mix together the dry ingredients then rub in the fat.
2. Press the mixture into a 25 x 30 cm (10 x 12 ins) Swiss roll tin.
3. Bake 150°C, 300°F, Gas 2, fan oven 130°C, for 40–45 mins.
4. Allow to cool slightly before cutting into pieces.

WALNUT BARS

1 medium egg   5 ml (1 tsp) vanilla essence
225 g (8 oz) butter   200 g (7 oz) plain flour
225 g (8 oz) caster sugar   50 g (2 oz) chopped walnuts

1. Separate the egg.
2. Cream butter and sugar. Mix in the egg yolk, vanilla essence and flour.
3. Press mixture into a greased oblong tin size 25 x 18 x 5 cm (10 x 7 x 2 ins).
4. Lightly whisk egg white and brush over mixture. Sprinkle on the walnuts.
5. Bake 180°C, 355°F, Gas 4, fan oven 160°C, for 40–50 mins.

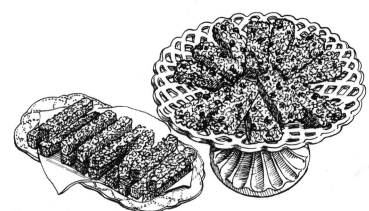

GOLDEN CRUNCH

Makes 16 fingers.

80 g (3 oz) margarine   60 ml (4 tbsp) golden syrup
25 g (1 oz) caster sugar   175 g (6 oz) oats

1. Place margarine, sugar and syrup in a saucepan. Melt gently then remove from heat and allow to cool for 5 mins.
2. Stir in the oats and mix well.
3. Spread into a greased and base-lined 20 cm (8 ins) square tin.
4. Bake 190°C, 375°F, Gas 5, fan oven 170°C, for 15–20 mins.
5. Cut into fingers whilst still warm.

FRUITY FLAPJACKS

Makes 12 bars.

115 g (4 oz) margarine   50 g (2 oz) raisins
115 g (4 oz) golden syrup   225 g (8 oz) oats
50 g (2 oz) demerara sugar

1. In a saucepan gently melt the margarine, syrup and sugar.
2. Stir in the raisins and oats mixing well.
3. Press mixture into a shallow 18 cm (7 ins) square tin.
4. Bake 180°C, 355°F, Gas 4, fan oven 160°C, for 25–35 mins until golden brown.
5. Cut into 12 bars whilst warm then place on wire rack to cool.

COCONUT BARS

These are ideal for packed lunch. They won't last long enough to worry about whether they'll remain fresh. Makes 24 bars.

115 g (4 oz) butter, softened
115 g (4 oz) caster sugar
2 medium eggs
5 ml (1 tsp) vanilla essence

175 g (6 oz) plain flour, sieved
80 g (3 oz) ground rice
115 g (4 oz) desiccated coconut

1. Place all the ingredients into a bowl and beat with a wooden spoon for 3 mins or in a mixer for one minute until a smooth dough is formed.
2. Spread the mixture evenly into a greased and base-lined 25 x18 cm (10 x 7 ins) shallow tin.
3. Chill for one hour.
4. Bake 160°C, 325°F, Gas 3, fan oven 140°C, for 35–45 mins until pale golden in colour.
5. Leave to cool for 5 mins then cut into 24 bars.

PITCAITHLY BANNOCK

Usually served for High Tea in Scotland. Makes one 18 cm (7 ins) round.

175 g (6 oz) plain flour
25 g (1 oz) ground rice
115 g (4 oz) butter
80 g (3 oz) caster sugar

25 g (1 oz) chopped mixed peel
25 g (1 oz) chopped mixed nuts
30 ml (2 tbsp) milk
caster sugar for sprinkling

1. In a bowl place the flour and ground rice. Add the butter and rub in until the mixture resembles fine breadcrumbs.
2. Stir in the sugar, peel and nuts. Add the milk and mix to a dough. Knead until smooth.
3. Place the mixture evenly into a greased and base-lined 18 cm (7 ins) sandwich tin. Press down firmly and prick all over.
4. Bake 160°C, 325°F, Gas 3, fan oven 140°C, for 35–45 mins until pale golden.
5. Leave to cool for 10 mins then cut into 8 wedges and sprinkle with sugar.
6. Cool on a wire rack.

VARIATION:
Replace 50 g (2 oz) plain flour for 50 g (2 oz) of oat flour.

DATE, CHOCOLATE AND NUT FLAPJACKS

Makes one 18 cm (7 ins) square tin.

225 g (8 oz) stoned dates, chopped
45 ml (3 tbsp) water
30 ml (2 tbsp) honey
finely grated zest of 1 orange
115 g (4 oz) margarine

50 g (2 oz) soft brown sugar
115 g (4 oz) plain wholemeal flour
115 g (4 oz) chocolate, grated
80 g (3 oz) rolled oats
50 g (2 oz) Brazil nuts, finely chopped

1. Place the chopped dates, water, honey and orange zest in a saucepan. Gently heat to melt the honey allowing the mixture to boil. Remove from the heat and leave to cool for 15 mins.
2. Place margarine and sugar in a small saucepan. Melt gently. Allow to cool.
3. Sieve the flour then stir in grated chocolate, oats and nuts mixing well. Stir in the melted mixture and blend together.
4. Press half the mixture into a greased and base-lined 18 cm (7 ins) square tin.
5. Spread the cooled date and honey mixture evenly over the base and sprinkle the remaining rubbed-in mixture. Press down gently.
6. Bake 180°C, 355°F, Gas 4, fan oven 160°C, for 40–50 mins.
7. Leave to cool before cutting into bars.

JIFFY FRUIT FINGERS

No mixing – just layer all the ingredients into the tin. Makes 33 fingers.

115 g (4 oz) butter or margarine
115 g (4 oz) oats
50 g (2 oz) glacé cherries,
   finely chopped

115 g (4 oz) sultanas
50 g (2 oz) chocolate chips
400 g (14 oz) can sweetened
   condensed milk

1. Gently melt the butter in a saucepan then pour into a Swiss roll tin approx. 30 x 23 cm (12 x 9 ins) and spread over the base.
2. Sprinkle the oats evenly on top then sprinkle the cherries, sultanas and chocolate chips.
3. Evenly pour over the condensed milk.
4. Bake 180°C, 355°F, Gas 4, fan oven 160°C, for 20–30 mins until golden in colour.
5. Cool in tin for 15 mins. Cut into 33 fingers. Leave in tin until completely cold.

RICH GINGER FLAPJACK

Makes 12 squares.

115 g (4 oz) butter

115 g (4 oz) granulated sugar

90 ml (6 tbsp) golden syrup

225 g (8 oz) oats

5 ml (1 tsp) ground ginger

1. Place the butter, sugar and the golden syrup in a saucepan and melt over a gentle heat.
2. Stir in the oats and ginger mixing well.
3. Place the mixture into a base-lined 18 cm (7 ins) square tin and press down evenly.
4. Bake 180°C (355°F), Gas 4, fan oven 160°C, for 25–35 mins until golden and set.
5. Cool then cut into 12 squares.

SYRUP OAT SLICES

Makes approx. 20.

Base:

80 g (3 oz) plain flour

80 g (3 oz) oats

80 g (3 oz) margarine

water to mix

Topping:

60 ml (4 tbsp) apricot jam

115 g (4 oz) margarine

175 g (6 oz) golden syrup

80 g (3 oz) oats

80 g (3 oz) desiccated coconut

few drops almond essence

1. Place the flour and the oats in a bowl then rub in the margarine to fine breadcrumbs.
2. Mix in enough water to form a firm dough. Roll out pastry and line a shallow 25 x 18 cm (10 x 7 ins) tin.
3. Spread the apricot jam over the pastry.
4. In a saucepan gently melt the margarine and syrup together.
5. Add the oats, coconut and essence mixing well.
6. Spread topping evenly over the jam.
7. Bake 180°C, 355°F, Gas 4, fan oven 160°C, for 30–40 mins until the mixture is golden.
8. When cool cut into slices.

SAVOURY BISCUITS

CRACKAMACS

Serve with cheese.

115 g (4 oz) self-raising flour   **milk or water to mix**
2.5 ml ($^1/_2$ tsp) salt

1. Sift the flour and salt into a basin. Add the milk or water and mix with a fork to make a dough.
2. Roll it out very thinly on a floured board and cut into rounds or squares.
3. Place on greased baking trays.
4. Bake 200°C, 400°F, Gas 6, fan oven 180°C, for 10–15 mins.

CURRY KNOTS

115 g (4 oz) plain flour, sieved   **pinch of salt**
50 g (2 oz) margarine   **egg yolk or water to mix**
10 ml (2 tsp) curry powder   **egg yolk to glaze**

1. Rub the fat into the flour. Add the sieved curry powder and salt mixing well.
2. Bind the mixture to a stiff but pliable dough with a little egg yolk or water.
3. Knead the dough well to remove any cracks and roll it into a long strip about 2 cm ($^3/_4$ inch) thick. Cut this into 15 cm (6 ins) long pieces and tie each one into a knot.
4. Place on greased baking trays. Brush them with beaten egg yolk.
5. Bake 180°C, 355°F, Gas 4, fan oven 160°C, 10–15 mins until golden.

DIGESTIVE BISCUITS

Serve with cheese.

175 g (6 oz) wholewheat flour
25 g (1 oz) oatmeal
5 ml (1 tsp) baking powder
2.5 ml (^{1}/$_2$ tsp) salt

80 g (3 oz) butter or margarine
40 g (1^1/$_2$ oz) soft brown sugar
30–45 ml (2–3 tbsp) milk

1. Mix together the flour and oatmeal. Sift in the baking powder and salt and rub in the fat.
2. Stir in the sugar. Add the milk and mix to a stiff dough.
3. Roll the dough out thinly and prick it well. Cut out 6 cm (2^1/$_2$ ins) rounds with a plain cutter.
4. Place on a baking tray.
5. Bake 190°C, 375°F, Gas 5, fan oven 170°C, for 15–20 mins.

WHOLEMEAL SAVOURY TITBITS

115 g (4 oz) wholemeal flour
2.5 ml (^{1}/$_2$ tsp) baking powder
pinch of salt

25 g (1 oz) lard
milk to mix

Topping:
60 ml (4 tbsp) cream cheese
15 ml (1 tbsp) grated cheese
15 ml (1 tbsp) chopped celery

salt, pepper and mustard to taste
parsley and red pepper to garnish

For the biscuits:
1. Sieve together the flour, baking powder and salt.
2. Rub in the lard then mix with enough milk to make a stiff dough.
3. Roll out very thinly. Prick the dough and cut into small rounds.
4. Place on greased baking trays.
5. Bake 180°C, 355°F, Gas 4, fan oven 160°C, for 10–15 mins until biscuits are firm and golden brown.
6. Allow to cool completely.
7. When they are cold store them in an airtight tin.

For the topping:
8. Mix all the ingredients and spread onto the biscuits. Garnish.

WALNUT SAVOURY BISCUITS

These are wonderful with a glass of dry sherry.

175 g (6 oz) plain flour
2.5 ml (1/2 tsp) salt, and pinch for glaze
2.5 ml (1/2 tsp) dry mustard
pinch of pepper
50 g (2 oz) rolled oats

80 g (3 oz) margarine
80 g (3 oz) Cheddar cheese, grated
50 g (2 oz) chopped walnuts
1 medium egg
150 ml (1/4 pint) cold water

1. Sieve together the dry ingredients. Add the oats and rub in the margarine.
2. Stir in the grated cheese and walnuts reserving a few chopped nuts.
3. Beat the egg and reserve a teaspoonful for the glaze. Add the egg to the mixture and bind to a stiff dough with the water.
4. Roll out the mixture and trim to make a rectangle. Add a pinch of salt to the remaining egg and brush over the surface. Sprinkle the top with a few chopped nuts.
5. Cut into shapes. Place on greased baking trays.
6. Bake 190°C, 375°F, Gas 5, fan oven 170°C, for 10–15 mins.
7. Leave to cool for 5 mins before removing to wire rack.

GUERNSEY BISCUITS

These are a cross between a sweet roll and a biscuit.

25 g (1 oz) fresh yeast
15 g (1/2 oz) caster sugar
225 ml (8 fl oz) warm milk or water

450 g (1 lb) plain flour
15 g (1/2 oz) salt
115 g (4 oz) margarine

1. Cream together the yeast and sugar. Add the liquid and leave this mixture in a warm place until it is frothy.
2. Sift the flour and salt and rub in the fat.
3. Add the yeast mixture to the flour and knead well.
4. Leave the dough covered to rise in a warm place for one hour.
5. Knock back the dough and knead again. Form into balls about 2 cm (3/4 inch) in diameter.
6. Flatten the balls and roll out. Place on greased baking trays and allow to prove for 15–20 mins in a warm place.
7. Bake 200°C, 400°F, Gas 6, fan oven 180°C, for 15–25 mins.
8. Cool completely. These can be frozen.

PAPRIKA CHEESE BISCUITS

175 g (6 oz) plain flour, sieved
175 g (6 oz) butter
80 g (3 oz) Cheddar cheese,
    finely grated
2.5 ml (^{1}/2 tsp) paprika

1 medium egg yolk
50 g (2 oz) almonds with skins on
beaten egg to glaze
paprika to finish

1. Rub the butter into the flour. Add the cheese, paprika and lightly beaten egg yolk.
2. Stir in the nuts and work the mixture to a smooth dough.
3. Roll out to a thickness of 1 cm (^{1}/2 inch). Cut out shapes with a small plain cutter.
4. Place on greased baking trays and brush tops with beaten egg and sprinkle lightly with paprika.
5. Bake 160°C, 325°F, Gas 3, fan oven 140°C, for 15–20 mins.

CHEESE SABLES

80 g (3 oz) plain flour
80 g (3 oz) butter
80 g (3 oz) mature Cheddar cheese, grated

salt and pepper to taste
1 medium egg

1. Sift the flour. Cut the butter into pieces and rub into the flour.
2. Add the cheese and season with the salt and pepper. Press the mixture together to make a dough.
3. Wrap the dough in greaseproof paper and chill in the fridge for about 30 mins.
4. Carefully roll out the dough until fairly thin. Cut into strips about 5 cm (2 ins) wide and brush with lightly beaten egg. Cut into triangles.
5. Place on a baking tray lined with greaseproof paper.
6. Bake 190°C, 375°F, Gas 5, fan oven 170°C, for 10–15 mins until sablés are golden.

CHEESE CRACKERS

115 g (4 oz) self-raising flour	cold water
pinch of salt ·	115 g (4 oz) butter or margarine
25 g (1 oz) Cheddar cheese, finely grated	

1. Sift the flour and salt into a basin then add the cheese.
2. Mix to a firm dough with the cold water and knead the mixture until smooth.
3. Roll into a 23 x 13 cm (9 x 5 ins) oblong. Mark into three portions. Spread 25 g (1 oz) of the butter over two-thirds of the dough and fold the unbuttered portion between the two buttered portions envelope fashion. Give the dough a half turn and roll again a little larger than the original oblong.
4. Repeat the process with the remainder of the butter and fold again then cover.
5. Put in a cool place for 30 mins.
6. Roll out and fold once again (with no fat) then roll to 5 mm ($^1/_4$ inch) thick.
7. Cut into squares. Prick all over.
8. Place on a greased baking tray.
9. Bake 160°C, 325°F, Gas 3, fan oven 140°C, for 15–25 mins.

CHEESE BISCUITS

These are wonderful with a selection of cheeses.

225 g (8 oz) plain flour	pinch of cayenne
80 g (3 oz) butter	225 g (8 oz) mature Cheddar cheese,
good pinch of salt	grated
5 ml (1 tsp) baking powder	1 medium egg yolk
	cold water

1. In a bowl rub the butter into the flour. Add the salt, baking powder, cayenne and grated cheese.
2. Beat the egg yolk with a little cold water and add it to the rest of the ingredients. Mix to a stiff dough.
3. Knead on a floured board. Roll out and stamp into rounds.
4. Place on a greased baking tray.
5. Bake 200°C, 400°F, Gas 6, fan oven 180°C, for 10–15 mins until pale golden in colour.

CHEESE STRAWS OR BISCUITS

50 g (2 oz) Cheddar cheese
2.5 ml (^{1}/2 tsp) salt
pinch of pepper

pinch of cayenne
80 g (3 oz) plain flour
50 g (2 oz) butter or margarine

1. Rub the cheese through a wire sieve. Add salt, pepper and cayenne to flour.
2. Partly cream the fat then add the cheese and the seasoned flour.
3. Mix to a paste and allow to stand for at least 30 mins.
4. Roll out on a lightly floured board and cut into straws or biscuits.
5. Place on a greased baking tray and prick with a fork.
6. Bake 180°C, 355°F, Gas 4, fan oven 160°C, for 10–15 mins.

BACON AND OATMEAL BISCUITS

115 g (4 oz) hard margarine
115 g (4 oz) rolled oats
115 g (4 oz) self-raising flour
salt and pepper

5 ml (1 tsp) dry mustard
80–115 g (3–4 oz) finely minced lean
    bacon
1 small egg, beaten

1. Rub margarine into the oats and flour. Add salt, pepper, mustard and bacon.
2. Mix together well before adding the beaten egg.
3. Roll the dough out fairly thinly and cut into shapes required.
4. Place on greased baking trays.
5. Bake 180°C, 355°F, Gas 4, fan oven 160°C, for 15–20 mins until golden brown.

OATCAKES

225 g (8 oz) plain flour
5 ml (1 tsp) salt
5 ml (1 tsp) bicarbonate of soda
15 ml (1 tbsp) caster sugar

450 g (1 lb) medium oatmeal
115 g (4 oz) margarine, melted
75 ml (5 tbsp) lukewarm water

1. Sift the flour, salt and bicarbonate of soda. Mix in the sugar and oatmeal and bind with the melted margarine and water.
2. Roll the dough out to a thickness of about 3 mm (^{1}/8 inch) and cut it out into 5 cm (2 ins) rounds.
3. Place on greased baking trays.
4. Bake 190°C, 375°F, Gas 5, fan oven 170°C, for 15–20 mins.

SWEET BISCUITS

CHOCOLATE GINGERBREAD PEOPLE

80 g (3 oz) dark brown sugar
50 g (2 oz) molasses sugar
80 g (3 oz) butter, softened
175 g (6 oz) self-raising flour

25 g (1 oz) cocoa powder
5 ml (1 tsp) ground ginger
5 ml (1 tsp) ground cinnamon
1 medium egg

Chocolate glaze:
105 ml (7 tbsp) water
115 g (4 oz) soft light brown sugar
115 g (4 oz) chocolate

To make gingerbread dough:
1. Place sugars and butter in a bowl. Beat until pale and creamy. Stir in the remaining ingredients and mix to a firm dough.
2. On a lightly floured surface roll out the dough to approx. 5 mm (¹/4 inch) thick. Cut out shapes.
3. Place shapes onto greased and lined baking trays.
4. Bake 180°C, 355°F, Gas 4, fan oven 160°C, for 10–15 mins.

To make chocolate glaze:
5. Place the water and sugar in a small saucepan then simmer over a gentle heat until sugar is dissolved. Remove from heat and add chocolate. Stir until melted. Allow to thicken. Spoon glaze over gingerbread shapes.

SHORTBREAD BISCUITS

My favourite biscuits. My sister Helen loves these also.

225 g (8 oz) butter
115 g (4 oz) icing sugar
225 g (8 oz) plain flour *and*
115 g (4 oz) cornflour, sieved together

pinch of salt
caster sugar for sprinkling

1. Cream fat and sugar thoroughly until soft and light.
2. Gradually work in flour, cornflour and salt. Knead until smooth.
3. Roll out mixture to 5 mm ($1/4$ inch) thick then cut into rounds, fingers or fancy shapes. Place on ungreased baking trays.
4. Bake 180°C, 355°F, Gas 4, fan oven 160°C, for 15–30 mins depending on shape and size.
5. Sprinkle with caster sugar then cool on wire racks.

EASTER BISCUITS

A traditional biscuit for Easter.

115 g (4 oz) butter
80 g (3 oz) caster sugar
1 medium egg, separated
200 g (7 oz) plain flour
pinch of salt
2.5 ml ($1/2$ tsp) mixed spice

2.5 ml ($1/2$ tsp) cinnamon
50 g (2 oz) currants
25 g (1 oz) chopped mixed peel
15–30 ml (1–2 tbsp) milk
a little caster sugar

1. Cream together the butter and sugar then beat in the egg yolk.
2. Sift together flour, salt and spices. Fold into creamed mixture with currants and peel.
3. Add enough milk to give a soft dough.
4. Knead lightly on a floured surface and roll out to 5 mm ($1/4$ inch) thick. Cut out using 6 cm ($2^1/2$ ins) fluted cutter.
5. Place on greased baking trays.
6. Bake 200°C, 400°F, Gas 6, fan oven 180°C, for 8–10 mins then brush with egg white and sprinkle with caster sugar. Return to oven for a further 8-10 mins.
7. Allow the biscuits to cool for a few minutes before placing on racks to cool completely.

BELGIAN SUGAR BISCUITS

80 g (3 oz) butter
150 g (5 oz) caster sugar
1 medium egg yolk

175 g (6 oz) plain flour, sieved
5 ml (1 tsp) ground ginger

1. Cream the butter and sugar together then add the egg yolk.
2. Add the sifted flour and ginger and mix thoroughly.
3. Shape the dough into a 6 cm (2¹/₂ ins) roll then wrap in greaseproof paper and chill in the fridge for a day.
4. Using a sharp knife cut the roll into thin slices of approximately 5 mm (¹/₄ inch).
5. Bake 160°C, 325°F, Gas 3, fan oven 140°C, for 15–20 mins until the biscuits are lightly browned.

BOURBON BISCUITS

115 g (4 oz) plain flour
2.5 ml (¹/₂ tsp) baking powder
15 g (¹/₂ oz) cocoa
50 g (2 oz) butter

50 g (2 oz) caster sugar
15 ml (1 tbsp) golden syrup
granulated sugar

Filling:
25 g (1 oz) plain chocolate
22.5 ml (1¹/₂ tbsp) water

50 g (2 oz) icing sugar

For the biscuits:
1. Sift together the flour, baking powder and cocoa.
2. Cream the butter and caster sugar until they are light and fluffy.
3. Beat in the syrup and stir in half of the flour mixture.
4. Turn the dough out onto a working surface and knead in the remaining flour mixture.
5. Roll out to a thickness of 5 mm (¹/₄ inch). Sprinkle with granulated sugar and press with a rolling pin.
6. Cut into neat fingers and place on greased baking trays.
7. Bake 160°C, 325°F, Gas 3, fan oven 140°C, for 15–20 mins.

For the filling:
8. Melt the chocolate in the water. Add the icing sugar and beat them together.
9. When the biscuits are cold sandwich together with the filling.

ALMOND AND LEMON BISCUITS

These scrummy biscuits are equally good made with orange instead of lemon.
Makes 18.

225 g (8 oz) plain flour
5 ml (1 tsp) baking powder
80 g (3 oz) caster sugar
50 g (2 oz) ground almonds

zest and juice of 1 lemon, finely grated
115 g (4 oz) butter, melted
1 medium egg, beaten
25 g (1 oz) flaked almonds

1. Sift the flour and baking powder into a mixing bowl. Stir in the sugar, ground almonds and lemon zest.
2. Mix together the lemon juice, melted butter and beaten egg. Make a well in the centre of the dry ingredients and pour in the melted butter mixture. Mix to form a soft dough.
3. Roll out on a lightly floured surface and stamp out using a 5 cm (2 ins) cutter. Press a few flaked almonds on top of each cookie.
4. Bake 190°C, 375°F, Gas 5, fan oven 170°C, for 12–15 mins.
5. Transfer to a wire rack to cool completely.

APPLEBY FAIRINGS

Traditionally made for Whit Monday events.

275 g (10 oz) butter
450 g (1 lb) plain flour
225 g (8 oz) caster sugar

pinch of salt
1 medium egg yolk

1. Rub the butter into the flour then add the sugar and salt.
2. Add in the egg yolk. Work the mixture into a dry dough.
3. Roll out to 5 mm (¼ inch) thick and cut into rounds. Impress the biscuits with a pattern or prick them all over.
4. Bake 180°C, 355°F, Gas 4, fan oven 160°C, for 20–25 mins.

CARAWAY BISCUITS

115 g (4 oz) margarine   5 ml (1 tsp) caraway seeds
50 g (2 oz) icing sugar   a little milk
175 g (6 oz) self-raising flour

1. Cream the margarine and the icing sugar. Add the flour and the caraway seeds.
2. Mix to a stiff paste with a little milk.
3. Roll the dough out to a thickness of 5 mm ($^1/4$ inch) then cut into shapes.
4. Bake 180°C, 355°F, Gas 4, fan oven 160°C, for 15 mins or until golden brown.

CHOCOLATE OAT BISCUITS

50 g (2 oz) lard   5 ml (1 tsp) golden syrup
50 g (2 oz) margarine   5 ml (1 tsp) bicarbonate of soda
115 g (4 oz) self-raising flour   5 ml (1 tsp) vanilla essence
115 g (4 oz) rolled oats   15 ml (1 tbsp) boiling water
80 g (3 oz) caster sugar

Filling: *Topping:*
50 g (2 oz) butter   50 g (2 oz) cooking chocolate, melted
115 g (4 oz) icing sugar
15 ml (1 tbsp) cocoa powder

For the biscuits:
1. Rub the lard and margarine into the mixed flour, oats and sugar.
2. Mix the remaining ingredients together and add to make a fairly soft mixture.
3. Knead the dough into a ball and put in the fridge for 30 mins.
4. Roll out and cut into rounds.
5. Bake 180°C, 355°F, Gas 4, fan oven 160°C, for 20 mins.
6. Leave to cool.

For the filling:
7. Cream the butter and sieved icing sugar together. Add the cocoa and beat the mixture well.
8. Sandwich the biscuits together in pairs with the filling and coat the tops with melted chocolate.

CURLY PETERS

Plain mixture:

115 g (4 oz) margarine
225 g (8 oz) plain flour
115 g (4 oz) caster sugar
5 ml (1 tsp) baking powder
1 medium egg

Chocolate mixture:

115 g (4 oz) margarine
175 g (6 oz) plain flour sieved with ...
50 g (2 oz) cocoa powder
115 g (4 oz) caster sugar
5 ml (1 tsp) baking powder
1 medium egg

For both mixtures:
1. Rub the margarine into the flour, and then add the sugar and baking powder.
2. Bind together with the egg to make a stiff paste.
3. Roll out each mixture separately then lay the chocolate mixture on top of the plain one.
4. Roll up like a Swiss roll. Cut the roll into 5 mm (¼ inch) slices and place on greased baking trays.
5. Bake 150°C, 300°F, Gas 2, fan oven 130°C, for 20–25 mins or until pale brown.

GARIBALDI BISCUITS

200 g (7 oz) self-raising flour
25 g (1 oz) cornflour
50 g (2 oz) caster sugar
pinch of salt
50 g (2 oz) butter or margarine

1 medium egg yolk
a little milk
80–115 g (3–4 oz) currants
caster sugar for sprinkling

1. Sieve the flour, cornflour, sugar and salt into a basin. Rub in the butter until the mixture is the consistency of breadcrumbs.
2. Mix to a stiffish dough with the egg yolk and milk.
3. Turn onto a floured board and roll out to a thin oblong.
4. Trim the edges then sprinkle one half of the dough with the currants. Fold over the other half of the dough and press the edges well together.
5. Roll the dough lightly with a floured rolling pin until it is about 3 mm (⅛ inch) thick. Cut into 5 cm (2 ins) squares.
6. Place on greased baking trays.
7. Bake 200°C, 400°F, Gas 6, fan oven 180°C, for 15 mins until golden.
8. Sprinkle with caster sugar.

CRESCENT BISCUITS

200 g (7 oz) plain flour
175 g (6 oz) fat
   (half butter, half margarine)
50 g (2 oz) caster sugar

80 g (3 oz) ground almonds
few drops of vanilla essence
caster sugar for sprinkling

1. Rub the flour and fat together.
2. Add the sugar, almonds and essence.
3. Knead the mixture to a stiff paste.
4. Roll out to a thickness of 1 cm ($^{1}/_{2}$ inch). Cut into crescent shapes.
5. Bake 150°C, 300°F, Gas 2, fan oven 130°C, for 30 mins.
6. Sprinkle with caster sugar.

OATMEAL BISCUITS

80 g (3 oz) butter
175 g (6 oz) coarse oatmeal
150 g (5 oz) plain flour

5 ml (1 tsp) baking powder
115 g (4 oz) caster sugar
a little milk

1. Rub the butter into the dry ingredients then add milk.
2. Roll out the dough and cut into shapes.
3. Place on a well-greased baking tray.
4. Bake 150°C, 300°F, Gas 2, fan oven 130°C, for 15–20 mins.

LEMON CRESCENTS

zest and juice of $^{1}/_{2}$ lemon
50 g (2 oz) caster sugar
50 g (2 oz) butter

100 g (4 oz) plain flour
1 medium egg
chopped almonds

1. Rub the grated lemon zest and the caster sugar in a basin until the sugar is yellow.
2. Rub the butter into the flour until it is free from lumps.
3. Add the lemon juice and sugar and sufficient egg to blend together.
4. Roll the dough out thinly and cut into crescent shapes.
5. Place on a greased baking tray. Brush over with beaten egg and sprinkle with chopped almonds.
6. Bake 180°C, 355°F, Gas 4, fan oven 160°C, for 20–25 mins.

NOVELTY BISCUITS

These make delightful treats at children's birthday parties.

50 g (2 oz) margarine	pinch of salt
50 g (2 oz) caster sugar	15 g (1/2 oz) chopped walnuts
115 g (4 oz) self-raising flour	15 g (1/2 oz) glacé cherries, chopped
10 ml (2 tsp) desiccated coconut	20 ml (4 tsp) beaten egg

1. Cream the margarine and sugar together until creamy.
2. Mix together the dry ingredients and gradually add the cherries to the creamed mixture.
3. Bind the dough together with the egg.
4. Roll out and cut into shapes.
5. Bake 180°C, 355°F, Gas 4, fan oven 160°C, for 15–20 mins.

MARZIPAN BISCUITS

Try these with coffee after dinner.

115 g (4 oz) caster sugar	few drops of almond essence
80 g (3 oz) ground almonds	25 g (1 oz) icing sugar
finely grated rind of 1 small orange	25 g (1 oz) finely flaked blanched
2 small egg yolks	almonds

1. Mix the caster sugar, ground almonds and orange rind together in a medium-sized bowl.
2. Make a well in the centre of the mixture and put in the egg yolks and almond essence.
3. Using a small spatula gradually work in the dry ingredients.
4. Lightly knead the mixture until it forms a smooth paste.
5. Shape into a ball. Wrap in greaseproof paper and chill in the fridge for 30 mins.
6. Sprinkle a board and rolling pin with icing sugar then roll the paste very thinly and carefully. Using a 5 cm (2 ins) cutter cut the marzipan into circles.
7. Place them spaced slightly apart on a large greased baking tray. Put a few almonds on each circle.
8. Bake 190°C, 375°F, Gas 5, fan oven 170°C, in the centre of the oven for 8–10 mins.
9. Cool on a wire rack.

SEMOLINA PYRAMID BISCUITS

80 g (3 oz) butter
50 g (2 oz) caster sugar
50 g (2 oz) cornflour

25 g (1 oz) semolina
a little jam

1. Cream the butter and sugar together.
2. Mix the cornflour and semolina and add to the creamed mixture. Knead well.
3. Roll the dough out thinly. Cut out equal numbers of rounds with a 2.5 cm (1 inch) fluted cutter, a 4 cm (1¹/₂ ins) plain cutter, and a 5 cm (2 ins) fluted cutter.
4. Put on greased baking trays.
5. Bake 180°C, 355°F, Gas 4, fan oven 160°C, for 15–20 mins.
6. When cold sandwich the three rounds together with jam to form pyramid shapes.

OAT BISCUITS

Makes 14.

115 g (4 oz) plain flour
pinch of salt
115 g (4 oz) oats
40 g (1¹/₂ oz) margarine

40 g (1¹/₂ oz) lard
50 g (2 oz) caster sugar
30 ml (2 tbsp) milk

1. Sieve the flour and salt into a bowl then stir in the oats and rub in the fat until the mixture resembles fine breadcrumbs.
2. Stir in the sugar. Add the milk and mix to a soft dough.
3. On a lightly floured surface roll out the dough to approx. 5 mm (¹/₄ inch) thick. Cut into 6 cm (2¹/₂ ins) rounds and place onto lightly greased baking trays.
4. Bake 180°C, 355°F, Gas 4, fan oven 160°C, for 15–20 mins until set and crisp.

SHREWSBURY BISCUITS

115 g (4 oz) butter
115 g (4 oz) caster sugar
1 medium egg
rind and juice of $^1/_2$ lemon

25 g (1 oz) currants
225 g (8 oz) plain flour
pinch of bicarbonate of soda

1. Cream the butter and sugar then add the egg, lemon rind and juice, currants, flour and bicarbonate of soda.
2. Knead well. Cover and leave the mixture in the fridge overnight.
3. Roll it out to a thickness of 5 mm ($^1/_4$ inch) and cut into rounds.
4. Bake 180°C, 355°F, Gas 4, fan oven 160°C, for 15–25 mins.

WHEATEN BISCUITS

115 g (4 oz) margarine
50 g (2 oz) caster sugar
50 g (2 oz) plain wholemeal flour

2.5 ml ($^1/_2$ tsp) salt
pinch bicarbonate of soda
115 g (4 oz) rolled oats

1. Cream together the margarine and sugar then gradually work in the flour, salt and bicarbonate of soda.
2. Turn mixture out onto floured board and sprinkle with the oats. Knead well.
3. Roll the dough out to a thickness of 1 cm ($^1/_2$ inch) and score with a fork to roughen the surface. Cut into shapes.
4. Place on greased baking trays.
5. Bake 190°C, 375°F, Gas 5, fan oven 170°C, for 15–20 mins until light and golden.

WHOLEMEAL SHORTCAKE

115 g (4 oz) butter
50 g (2 oz) dark brown sugar
225 g (8 oz) plain wholemeal flour

25 g (1 oz) ground almonds
pinch of salt
$^1/_2$ medium egg yolk

1. Cream the butter and sugar until they are soft and creamy.
2. Stir in the dry ingredients then add the egg yolk.
3. Form the dough into rounds or roll out and cut into shapes.
4. Place on greased baking trays.
5. Bake 160°C, 325°F, Gas 3, fan oven 140°C, for 15–20 mins until golden brown.

KELVIN CRISPS

115 g (4 oz) plain flour	80 g (3 oz) caster sugar
2.5 ml (^{1}/2 tsp) ground cinnamon	80 g (3 oz) desiccated coconut
2.5 ml (^{1}/2 tsp) baking powder	1 medium egg
115 g (4 oz) butter or margarine	

1. Sieve the flour, cinnamon and baking powder into a bowl then rub in the butter.
2. Add the remainder of the dry ingredients and mix together with the well-beaten egg to make a fairly stiff dough.
3. Roll the dough out to a thickness of 5 mm (^{1}/4 inch). Stamp out into small rounds and place on a greased baking tray.
4. Bake 180°C, 355°F, Gas 4, fan oven 160°C, for 15 mins.

VARIATIONS:
When they are cold serve them:
i. Plain.
ii. Topped with a dab of melted chocolate and half a glacé cherry.
iii. Sandwiched together with apricot jam.

CHOCOLATE STARS

These are lovely served with a mug of hot chocolate.

225 g (8 oz) plain flour	115 g (4 oz) caster sugar
25 g (1 oz) cornflour	1 medium egg
15 g (^{1}/2 oz) cocoa powder	2.5 ml (^{1}/2 tsp) vanilla essence
pinch of salt	10 ml (2 tsp) milk
115 g (4 oz) butter	chocolate drops for topping

1. Sieve the flour, cornflour, cocoa and salt into a bowl.
2. Cream the butter and sugar until they are light and fluffy.
3. Beat in the egg and vanilla essence.
4. Work in the flour mixture and mix to a soft dough with the milk.
5. Put mixture into a large forcing bag fitted with a large star nozzle. Pipe stars 4 cm (1^1/2 ins) in diameter and spaced well apart on greased baking trays.
6. Place a chocolate drop in the centre of each star.
7. Bake 160°C, 325°F, Gas 3, fan oven 140°C, for 15 mins.
8. Cool on a wire rack.

VIENNESE FINGERS

175 g (6 oz) margarine
50 g (2 oz) caster sugar
175 g (6 oz) self-raising flour, sieved
2.5 ml (¹/2 tsp) vanilla essence

To finish:
60 ml (4 tbsp) jam
80 g (3 oz) chocolate, melted

1. Cream the margarine and sugar together then stir in the flour and vanilla essence mixing well.
2. Place the mixture into a piping bag with a star nozzle and pipe 7.5 cm (3 ins) lengths onto greased baking trays.
3. Bake 160°C, 325°F, Gas 3, fan oven 140°C, for 15–25 mins until pale golden.
4. Allow to cool slightly on baking trays before placing on cooling racks to cool completely.
5. **To finish:** Sandwich biscuits together with jam and dip ends into the melted chocolate.

BUFTON BISCUITS

150 g (5 oz) margarine
115 g (4 oz) granulated sugar
115 g (4 oz) self-raising flour
25 g (1 oz) semolina
115 g (4 oz) rolled oats

30 ml (2 tbsp) golden syrup
pinch of salt
5 ml (1 tsp) baking powder
5 ml (1 tsp) bicarbonate of soda
10 ml (2 tsp) milk

Filling:
50 g (2 oz) butter
115 g (4 oz) icing sugar

5 ml (1 tsp) cocoa powder
5 ml (1 tsp) coffee essence

For the biscuits:
1. Cream the margarine and sugar together until creamy.
2. Add the flour, semolina, oats, syrup, salt and baking powder.
3. Add the bicarbonate of soda mixed with the milk.
4. Make small rough balls and place on greased baking trays.
5. Bake 180°C, 355°F, Gas 4, fan oven 160°C, for 15–20 mins until set.
6. When the biscuits are cold serve plain or sandwich them with the filling.

For the filling:
7. Cream butter until soft. Gradually add the sieved icing sugar and cream them together. Add the cocoa powder and coffee essence and beat the mixture well.

ORANGE FORK BISCUITS

Traditional biscuits with an orange flavour. Why not try one of the variations as well? Makes 24.

175 g (6 oz) butter, softened
80 g (3 oz) caster sugar

grated zest of 1 orange
225 g (8 oz) self-raising flour

1. Cream the butter, sugar and orange zest together then mix in the flour.
2. Form to a soft dough with hands.
3. Place walnut sized pieces of the dough onto well-greased baking trays allowing room for spreading.
4. Dip a fork in a little cold water and flatten the biscuits.
5. Bake 180°C, 355°F, Gas 4, fan oven 160°C, for 15–20 mins until pale golden.
6. Place on cooling rack to cool completely.

   VARIATIONS:
   Use zest of 1 lemon or replace 25 g (1 oz) of flour with cocoa.

SWEET PRETZELS

These remind me of the pretzels served in Holland.

25 g (1 oz) butter
1 medium egg
50 g (2 oz) icing sugar
115 ml (4 fl oz) double cream

150 g (5 oz) plain flour
1 medium egg white lightly beaten
icing sugar for sprinkling

1. Beat butter with egg, icing sugar and cream. Work in flour to form a soft dough.
2. Wrap and chill for 30 mins.
3. Break off pieces the size of walnuts and roll them into sausage shapes.
4. Shape into twisted figures of eight.
5. Place on greased baking trays and brush with beaten egg white.
6. Bake 200°C, 400°F, Gas 6, fan oven 180°C, for 15–20 mins.
7. Cool then sprinkle with icing sugar.

   VARIATION:
   Divide dough into two. Flavour one half with cinnamon then twist dough together.

ABBEY BISCUITS

150 g (5 oz) margarine
150 g (5 oz) caster sugar
15 ml (1 tbsp) milk
5 ml (1 tsp) bicarbonate of soda

5 ml (1 tsp) golden syrup
150 g (5 oz) plain flour
115 g (4 oz) rolled oats

1. Cream the margarine and sugar together then add the milk, bicarbonate of soda and syrup.
2. Stir in the flour and oats and mix well.
3. Roll the dough into small balls and space them evenly apart on a baking tray.
4. Bake 150°C, 300°F, Gas 2, fan oven 130°C, for 25 mins until golden brown.

FLAKED ALMOND BISCUITS

115 g (4 oz) margarine or butter
115 g (4 oz) caster sugar
10 ml (2 tsp) black treacle
115 g (4 oz) self-raising flour

115 g (4 oz) rolled oats
25 g (1 oz) flaked almonds
5 ml (1 tsp) bicarbonate of soda
60 ml (4 tbsp) boiling water

1. Cream the butter and sugar. Add the treacle then mix in the flour, oats and nuts.
2. Dissolve the bicarbonate of soda in the water and stir into the mixture.
3. Roll teaspoonfuls of the mixture into balls. Place on greased baking trays allowing room for the biscuits to spread.
4. Bake 180°C, 355°F, Gas 4, fan oven 160°C, for 15–20 mins.

COCONUT BUTTER BISCUITS

175 g (6 oz) butter or margarine
30 ml (2 tbsp) golden syrup
115 g (4 oz) desiccated coconut

225 g (8 oz) self-raising flour
2.5 ml (^{1}/2 tsp) bicarbonate of soda
175 g (6 oz) caster sugar

1. Gently melt the butter and syrup in a pan and add the coconut.
2. Sieve the flour and bicarbonate of soda into the mixture. Stir in the sugar mixing well.
3. Shape the dough into small balls and place on greased baking trays leaving room for the biscuits to spread.
4. Bake 180°C, 355°F, Gas 4, fan oven 160°C, for 12–15 mins.

ALMOND BALLS

Ideal to keep in case of unexpected visitors.

115 g (4 oz) butter or margarine
115 g (4 oz) caster sugar
115 g (4 oz) ground almonds
1 medium egg separated

5 ml (1 tsp) vanilla essence
115 g (4 oz) plain flour
flaked almonds

1. Cream the butter and sugar together.
2. Stir in the ground almonds, yolk of the egg, vanilla essence and flour.
3. Knead the dough until it is well blended.
4. Roll it into small balls about 2.5 cm (1 inch) in diameter. Press a flaked almond on top of each one and brush them with the slightly beaten white of the egg. Place on greased baking trays.
5. Bake 170°C, 340°F, Gas 3, fan oven 150°C, for 10–12 mins.
6. Allow to cool for 5 mins on baking trays then cool on wire rack.

Note:
The butter and almonds will keep these biscuits fresh for several weeks in an airtight container.

ALMOND BUTTER CRISPS

These light-as-air biscuits are often served in Denmark with coffee.

200 g (7 oz) butter or margarine
175 g (6 oz) caster sugar
5 ml (1 tsp) vanilla essence

5 ml (1 tsp) bicarbonate of soda
225 g (8 oz) self-raising flour
flaked almonds

1. Cream the butter and sugar until creamy. Add the vanilla essence.
2. Sieve the bicarbonate of soda with the flour and add to other ingredients.
3. Knead the dough together.
4. Roll into balls the size of a walnut.
5. Arrange on greased baking trays leaving room for the biscuits to flatten and spread.
6. Top each one with an almond flake.
7. Bake 180°C, 355°F, Gas 4, fan oven 160°C, for 15 mins or until golden brown.
8. Cool on trays for 5 mins before removing to a wire rack.

CHOCOLATE NUT BISCUITS

115 g (4 oz) butter	40 g (1¹/2 oz) chopped walnuts
175 g (6 oz) caster sugar	2.5 ml (¹/2 tsp) cream of tartar
1 medium egg	2.5 ml (¹/2 tsp) bicarbonate of soda
40 g (1¹/2 oz) chocolate, grated	few drops of vanilla essence
225 g (8 oz) plain flour	pinch of salt

1. Cream the butter and the sugar together.
2. Beat in the egg then add all the other ingredients. Blend well.
3. Form the dough into a roll about 4 cm (1¹/2 ins) in diameter and place in the fridge for about one hour.
4. When it is thoroughly chilled cut into slices with a sharp knife.
5. Place on greased baking trays.
6. Bake 180°C, 355°F, Gas 4, fan oven 160°C, for 10–15 mins.

DANISH SPECIER BISCUITS

175 g (6 oz) butter or margarine	25 g (1 oz) blanched chopped almonds
225 g (8 oz) plain flour	granulated sugar
80 g (3 oz) icing sugar	

1. Place butter, flour, sifted icing sugar and almonds into a bowl and mix together.
2. Shape the dough into two sausages about 5 cm (2 ins) thick and roll in granulated sugar until completely covered.
3. Place in a fridge until firm.
4. Cut the dough into 5 mm (¹/4 inch) thick slices and arrange on an ungreased baking tray.
5. Bake 200°C, 400°F, Gas 6, fan oven 180°C, for 8–10 mins until light brown around the edges.

HIGHLANDERS

50 g (2 oz) icing sugar, sieved

80 g (3 oz) plain flour

115 g (4 oz) butter

25 g (1 oz) demerara sugar

80 g (3 oz) self-raising flour

1. Cream icing sugar and butter until very light. Work in flours and knead well.
2. Form the mixture into a sausage shape and roll it in the demerara sugar.
3. Wrap the dough in greaseproof paper. Put in the fridge for at least one hour.
4. Cut into 5 mm (1/4 inch) slices and place on an ungreased baking tray.
5. Bake 180°C, 355°F, Gas 4, fan oven 160°C, for approx. 10 mins being careful not to burn the edges. Cool on a tray.

HONEY BISCUITS

50 g (2 oz) unsalted butter

5 ml (1 tsp) bicarbonate of soda

20 ml (4 tsp) clear honey

115 g (4 oz) plain flour, sieved

50 g (2 oz) caster sugar

25 g (1 oz) sugar lumps

1. Melt the butter and pour into a large bowl.
2. As it begins to cool stir in the honey, caster sugar and soda.
3. Add the sifted flour gradually and mix to a firm dough.
4. Divide into 16 pieces and roll into balls on a floured board.
5. Coarsely crush the sugar lumps and dip the top of each ball into this.
6. Place the balls on two baking trays lined with non-stick baking parchment.
7. Bake 200°C, 400°F, Gas 6, fan oven 180°C, for 8–12 mins.

LACE BISCUITS

115 g (4 oz) margarine

115 g (4 oz) chopped almonds

115 g (4 oz) caster sugar

50 g (2 oz) plain flour

juice of 1 lemon

pinch of salt

1. Cream the margarine, sugar and lemon juice together.
2. Add the almonds. Stir in the flour and salt. Mix the dough well.
3. Break off pieces the size of a walnut and put on greased baking trays. Space well apart to allow for spreading. Press with a fork.
4. Bake 180°C, 355°F, Gas 4, fan oven 160°C, for 15–20 mins.
5. Do not remove from trays until cold.

VANILLA KIPFERL

225 g (8 oz) butter
225 g (8 oz) plain flour
pinch of salt
5 ml (1 tsp) vanilla essence

115 g (4 oz) ground almonds or hazelnuts
or a mixture of half and half
115 g (4 oz) caster sugar
sieved icing or caster sugar for coating

1. Work the butter into the flour, salt, essence, nuts and caster sugar until a dough is formed.
2. Pinch off pieces the size of a walnut and roll into 'pencils' about 2 cm (³/4 inch) thick and 6 cm (2¹/2 ins) long then bend into a crescent.
3. When forming the biscuits try not to use any more flour as this will cause them to toughen.
4. Arrange on ungreased baking trays leaving about 2.5 cm (1 inch) between each biscuit as they do spread.
5. Bake 160°C, 325°F, Gas 3, fan oven 140°C, for 20–25 mins until the biscuits are pale golden.
6. Leave when cooked for 3 mins to firm up and dip in icing or caster sugar. Cool completely.

DIPPING BISCUITS

Adult biscuits ideal for serving with a glass of liqueur at the end of a special dinner. If you want to treat yourself at other times as well try with ice cream and hot chocolate sauce. Makes 12.

225 g (8 oz) plain flour
pinch of salt
2.5 ml (1 tsp) baking powder
80 g (3 oz) caster sugar

50 g (2 oz) chocolate chips
50 g (2 oz) ground almonds
2 medium eggs, beaten

1. Sieve into a bowl the flour, salt and baking powder. Stir in the sugar, chocolate chips and nuts.
2. Gradually add the eggs until a stiff dough forms.
3. Divide the dough into two and form each into a sausage shape, approx. 2.5 cm (1 inch) thick and 18 cm (7 ins) long.
4. Cut each into six slices and place on greased baking trays.
5. Bake 140°C, 285°F, Gas Mark 1, fan oven 120°C, for 35–45 mins until golden.
6. Allow to cool completely on wire rack.

JUMBLES

175 g (6 oz) butter
225 g (8 oz) plain flour
225 g (8 oz) caster sugar

grated rind of 1 lemon
1 large egg
caster sugar for dusting

1. Rub the butter into the flour. Add the sugar and lemon rind and stir in the beaten egg. Mix to a dough.
2. Roll the dough into long rolls.
3. Cut into 10 cm (4 ins) lengths and make them into wheel or 'S' shapes.
4. Bake 180°C, 355°F, Gas 4, fan oven 160°C, for 15–20 mins or until evenly browned.
5. Dust with caster sugar immediately.

TUILLES

1 medium egg white
100 g (3¹/₂ oz) caster sugar
grated zest of ¹/₂ lemon

40 g (1¹/₂ oz) plain flour
15 g (¹/₂ oz) ground almonds
50 g (2 oz) melted butter

1. Whisk egg white until stiff. Add sugar, re-whisk, then add the lemon rind.
2. Mix together the flour and ground almonds and fold into the mixture along with the melted butter.
3. Place half-teaspoonfuls of the mixture on greased baking trays leaving space between each one.
4. Bake 190°C, 375°F, Gas 5, fan oven 170°C, for 5–10 mins.
5. While tuilles are still warm lay over a greased rolling pin to make them curl.
6. Serve with a rich party dessert.

GINGER BISCUITS

These biscuits become deliciously crisp on cooling.

115 g (4 oz) margarine
115 g (4 oz) caster sugar
15 ml (1 tbsp) black treacle
15 ml (1 tbsp) golden syrup

225 g (8 oz) self-raising flour
5 ml (1 tsp) ground ginger
5 ml (1 tsp) bicarbonate of soda
a little hot water

1. Cream the margarine and sugar in a bowl.
2. Warm the treacle and syrup and add to the creamed mixture with the sieved flour and ginger.
3. Dissolve the bicarbonate of soda in a little hot water and stir into the mixture. Mix well.
4. Roll the dough into balls and place on greased baking trays.
5. Bake 180°C, 355°F, Gas 4, fan oven 160°C, for 15 mins.
6. Cool on wire racks.

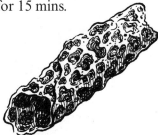

GINGER SNAPS

115 g (4 oz) margarine
60 ml (4 tbsp) golden syrup
225 g (8 oz) plain flour
pinch of salt
5 ml (1 tsp) ground ginger

115 g (4 oz) caster sugar
1 medium egg yolk
2.5 ml (1/2 tsp) bicarbonate of soda
a little milk

1. In a small saucepan melt the margarine and the golden syrup gently together.
2. Sieve the flour, salt and ginger into a basin and stir in the sugar.
3. Blend the mixture with the melted margarine and syrup and the beaten egg yolk.
4. Dissolve bicarbonate of soda in a little warm milk and add to mixture.
5. Turn the dough onto a floured board and knead until smooth.
6. Roll out thinly on a sugared board and cut into rounds approx. 5 cm (2 ins).
7. Place on a greased and floured baking tray.
8. Bake 190°C, 375°F, Gas 5, fan oven 170°C, for 15–20 mins.
9. Allow to set on the baking tray then leave to cool on a wire rack.
10. Store in an airtight container.

MICROWAVE ONLY

When cooking in the microwave it is important to remember:

1. All cooking utensils will get hot so always take care when removing from the microwave.
2. Check the wattage of your microwave. The minimum time given is for 850 watts and the maximum time is for 650 watts .
3. Check the food during cooking regularly.
4. If you do not know the wattage follow the minimum time given and add additional time as necessary.
5. Allow the food to stand at the end of the cooking time to complete cooking before removing from cooking dish to cool.

FLAPJACKS

Makes one 20 cm (8 ins) round.

45 ml (3 tbsp) golden syrup	**225 g (8 oz) rolled oats**
115 g (4 oz) soft brown sugar	**5 ml (1 tsp) baking powder**
115 g (4 oz) margarine	**1 medium egg, beaten**

1. Place syrup, sugar and margarine in a bowl. Microwave on MEDIUM for 1–2 mins until melted. Stir well.
2. Mix in the oats, baking powder and egg.
3. Place the mixture evenly into a 20 cm (8 ins) round microwave dish.
4. Cook on HIGH for 2–5 mins depending on the wattage of the microwave.
5. Allow to stand for about 10 mins to set. Cut into wedges to serve.

SPICY CURRANT ROUNDS

Makes 30.

225 g (8 oz) plain flour   115 g (4 oz) currants
5 ml (1 tsp) mixed spice   115 g (4 oz) demerara sugar
175 g (6 oz) butter

1. In a bowl sieve the flour and spice together. Rub in the butter until mixture resembles fine breadcrumbs. Stir in the currants and sugar.
2. Knead to a firm dough.
3. Shape dough into two sausage shapes approx. 15 cm (6 ins).
4. Cut each roll into 15 slices.
5. Place six at a time on greased greaseproof paper and microwave on HIGH for 1–3 mins depending on wattage of microwave.
6. Allow to stand for 2 mins then cool completely.

OATY CHOCOLATE BISCUITS

Try different chocolate coatings, plain, milk or white, for a change.

115 g (4 oz) butter   115 g (4 oz) rolled oats
50 g (2 oz) plain wholemeal flour   25 g (1 oz) dark brown sugar
50 g (2 oz) self raising flour   60 ml (4 tbsp) milk
2.5 ml (1/2 tsp) bicarbonate of soda

To finish:
115 g (4 oz) chocolate

1. In a large microwave bowl melt the butter on MEDIUM for approx. 45–60 seconds.
2. Mix in the remaining ingredients and form a soft dough.
3. On a lightly floured surface roll out the dough to 5 mm (1/4 inch) thick and cut out 5 cm (2 ins) rounds.
4. Place six at a time on greaseproof paper. Microwave on HIGH for 1–3 mins until cooked.
5. Allow the biscuits to stand for 5 mins before placing on wire rack to cool completely.
6. Break chocolate into pieces and place in a small microwave bowl. Melt on MEDIUM for 2–3 mins until melted. Dip cooled biscuits in chocolate.

CHOCOLATE BISCUITS

Makes 24

225 g (8 oz) butter, softened
115 g (4 oz) dark brown sugar
5 ml (1 tsp) vanilla essence

225 g (8 oz) self raising flour, sieved
50 g (2 oz) drinking chocolate, sieved

1. Cream the butter, sugar and essence until light and fluffy.
2. Stir flour and drinking chocolate into the mixture and form a soft dough.
3. Shape into 24 balls then flatten slightly.
4. Place six at a time on greased greaseproof paper. Microwave on HIGH for 1–2$\frac{1}{2}$ mins depending on the wattage of microwave.
5. Allow to stand for 2 mins then cool completely.

PEANUT COOKIES

Makes 36

115 g (4 oz) butter, softened
225 g (8 oz) dark brown sugar
115 g (4 oz) crunchy peanut butter

1 medium egg, beaten
175 g (6 oz) plain flour sieved together *with*
2.5 ml ($\frac{1}{2}$ tsp) baking powder

1. Cream the butter and sugar together until soft and lighter in colour. Beat in the peanut butter and egg.
2. Stir in the flour and baking powder mixing well to form a soft dough.
3. Shape the mixture into balls then flatten slightly.
4. Place six at a time on greased greaseproof paper and microwave on HIGH for 1–3 mins depending on the wattage of microwave.
5. Allow to stand for 5 mins then cool.

LEMON THINS

Makes 16

50 g (2 oz) butter, softened
50 g (2 oz) caster sugar
grated zest and juice of $\frac{1}{2}$ lemon

1 medium egg yolk
115 g (4 oz) plain flour, sieved

1. Cream the butter, sugar and lemon zest together until light and fluffy.
2. Stir in lemon juice and egg yolk.
3. Fold in the flour to form a stiff dough. Knead gently until smooth.
4. Shape dough into a sausage shape approx. 13 cm (5 ins) long. Wrap in greaseproof paper and chill for one hour.
5. Cut into slices, place eight onto greased greaseproof paper. Cook on HIGH for 1–2$\frac{1}{2}$ mins depending on wattage of microwave.
6. When cooked roll around handle of a wooden spoon. Allow to cool.

INGREDIENTS INDEX

INGREDIENTS INDEX

INGREDIENTS INDEX

INGREDIENTS INDEX

INGREDIENTS INDEX

INGREDIENTS INDEX

ABOUT THE WI

If you have enjoyed this book, the chances are that you would enjoy belonging to the largest women's organisation in the country – the National Federation of Women's Institutes, or the WI as it is usually known.

We are friendly, go-ahead, like-minded women, who derive enormous satisfaction from all the movement has to offer. The list is long – you can make new friends, have fun and companionship, visit new places, develop new skills, take part in community services, fight local campaigns, become a WI Market producer, and play an active rôle in an organisation that has a national voice.

The WI is the only women's organisation in the country that owns an adult education establishment. At Denman College, you can take a course in anything from car maintenance to paper sculpture, from book binding to yoga, or cordon bleu cookery to fly fishing.

For more information, write to the **National Federation of Women's Institutes, 104 New Kings Road, London SW6 4LY, phone 0171-371-9300. The NFWI email address is <hq@nfwi.org.uk>. The NFWI website is at <http://www.nfwi.org.uk> The NFWI Wales Office is at 19 Cathedral Road, Cardiff CF1 9LJ, phone 01222-221712.**

For more information and a catalogue about WI Books, contact WI Books, Glebe House, Church Street, Crediton, Devon EX17 2AF, phone 01363 777575

ABOUT THE AUTHOR

JILL BRAND is currently the NFWI Home Economics Adviser, based at the NFWI Unit, Denman College. Her rôle is to give professional support and advice to Federations and Members on all aspects of Home Economics. She is a member of Bucknell WI, Oxfordshire.

Jill was previously employed in the domestic appliance industry where she was involved in design, development and testing of products to ensure the consumers' needs were met. She also developed, tested and wrote recipes for recipe books, leaflets and magazines as well as being involved in the production of consumer booklets. She is the author of the *WI Book of Cakes*.

Jill is a Fellow of the Institute of Home Economics.

In her spare time, she enjoys gardening, collecting antiques, reading and researching the history of food – and, of course, cooking.

MORNFLAKE
Milling Oats since 1675

Not many companies today can trace their history back to 325 years before the current millennium began, but Mornflake can, having first milled oats in the beautiful Cheshire countryside for local farmers in 1675!

Today, 14 generations later, the company is still independently owned and managed by the direct descendants of those millers. With expertise and skills handed down from fathers to sons, this unparalleled experience ensures that you can continue to enjoy oat products of the highest possible quality from Mornflake.

No wonder Mornflake Oats regularly win the European milling industry's top International Gold Medals for quality, purity and consistency. The way Mornflake mill oats carefully retains the whole grain containing both germ and bran, only removing the inedible outer husk. Modern technology at this 'state of the art' mill is so sophisticated that the grain can be precisely sorted for shape, size and moisture so it is optimised for each of the many types of oat product produced by Mornflake.

TYPES OF OATS

Oats are an extremely versatile cereal and are available from Mornflake in many grades for breakfasts and cooking:

Rolled/Flaked Oats. Rolled oats are given many different names but are basically the same type of product. Mornflake produce them under the name 'SuperFast Oats'; flaked oats, oatflakes, quick oats, easy oats and porridge oats are some of the more common names also used. They are partially cooked during the milling process and are ideal for making porridge, muesli and flapjack biscuits.

MORNFLAKE
Milling Oats since 1675

Jumbo Oats are the largest variety of flaked oat and are ideal for making a good thick porridge with a more pronounced texture. They have a slightly nutty flavour and make superb biscuits. 'Mornflake Organic Oats' are made from oats specially grown to the established organic standards laid down by the U.K. Register of Organic Food Standards by which the crops rely for their purity on the goodness of the soil, enriched only by natural means.

Every oat crop under contract for Mornflake Oats is grown to the strictest standards by farmers who use traditional farming methods without any chemical fertilisers.

Medium Oatmeal is made from ground whole grain oats and has a pleasant slightly rough texture, ideal for porridge, oatcakes and parkin. It is the best variety for coating fish and meat before frying and is good in stuffings and crumble toppings.

Fine Oatmeal makes a lovely smooth milk pudding. This is the type to use as a thickening agent for soups, sauces and gravy.

Coarse Oatmeal is, as its name suggests, similar to medium oatmeal but is ground to a coarser grade for extra texture.

Pinhead Oatmeal can be made into delicious, traditional Scottish porridge which is more granular than the porridge most people are used to. Pinhead oatmeal is the 'chunkiest' grade of oatmeal in general usage and can be ideal for adding texture as well as nutritional value to soups, stews and toppings for pies and puddings.

Oat Bran is milled from the two thin layers which are found beneath the outer husk or 'hull' of the oat grain and they are particularly rich in soluble fibre. It makes a very smooth porridge and can be sprinkled into many recipes including cereals and salad dishes or used in baking for higher fibre food.

Oat flour is a very fine, smooth textured flour. Ideal as a baby food, it also makes a good thickening agent. Mixed with wheat flour it is delicious in biscuits, bread, cakes, scones and pastry. Oat flour is not as readily available in supermarkets as other products but it is easy to make your own. Simply place some Mornflake oats or fine or medium Mornflake oatmeal in a liquidiser or food processor and grind to flour. Keep a jar ready made up to add power to your cooking!

OATS AND YOUR HEALTH

The more you look into what oats have to offer, the more you begin to realize what an incredibly useful and beneficial cereal this is. They certainly add a delicious and healthy new dimension to baking biscuits.

MORNFLAKE
Milling Oats since 1675

It was dietary fibre which first began to interest the health-conscious eater. Two types of fibre are to be found in Mornflake Oats.

Soluble Fibre: This is the part of the fibre that can be more readily absorbed into the body through digestion. Science now shows it can play an important rôle in reducing harmful levels of cholesterol in the blood that can lead to heart attacks, provided of course that it is eaten as part of a low-fat diet.

Insoluble Fibre: This part adds 'roughage' to the diet, providing important bulk in the digestive system. This prevents the build-up of destructive chemicals that can lead to intestinal problems so common in today's 'fast food' society.

OATS FOR ENERGY

One of the perennial problems facing those who want to stay slim is the energy gap that often occurs between breakfast and lunchtime. This is when most people crave a quick and sweet snack as their body tells them to replenish its energy reserves. Mornflake Oats are low in fat yet the high content of complex carbohydrates and soluble fibre they contain help to sustain energy levels right through the morning and ward off those hunger pangs for longer. So if you can't have any oats at breakfast time and need some 'elevenses', oaty biscuits will do nicely!

Oats have also long been recognised as having a higher protein content than any other cereal (11.8%). Much of this protein, together with the important vitamins and minerals, come from the oat germ. The way Mornflake mill oats carefully retains the whole grain containing both germ and bran, only removing the inedible outer husk.

Other research on oats has indicated that they are good for the skin, help fend off cancers and help protect your body against ageing. Mornflake Oats are rich in biotin (vitamin H), a deficiency of which can cause hair loss. They are not unique in many of these benefits, but together they make a powerful argument for eating oats regularly.

With superb taste, versatility, nutritional value and value for money, this could be the ultimate health food! They make superb biscuits too!

For further information, visit our website at www.MornflakeOats.com